FREEDOM TO BELIEVE

*Personhood and Freedom
in Orthodox Christian
Ontology.*
ARCHBISHOP LAZAR PUHALO

SYNAXIS PRESS
The Canadian Orthodox Publishing House
**37323 HAWKINS ROAD,
DEWDNEY, B.C., V0M-1H0, Canada.**

ISBN:
Copyright 2017

DEDICATION
To Reader Andrew Bingham
who inspired the writing of this work

CONTENTS

FOREWORD
by David J. Goa
Canadian philosopher and educator

This is one of those rare books I wish I had written. For a number of years I have talked about the sympathy Orthodoxy and Existentialism (from Kierkegaard to Sartre) share in their critique of essentialism and their understanding of the human nature and our struggle for authenticity. This book signals a new departure for dialogue between contemporary thought and Orthodox sources of understanding. All too often, attempts by Orthodox thinkers to consider Existentialism have been grounded in an unwarranted fear as if their faith needed protecting. Archbishop Lazar, out of his vocation as teacher and shepherd, has engaged Existentialism with ease and grace, drawing out its gift as an antidote to both Christian and secular philosophies that for centuries have focused on questions which cloud Socrates' ancient and enduring call to "know thyself." This call is central to all human aspiration and, in particular, to the call of the Gospel of Jesus Christ. As Scripture makes clear, this call is never answered in the abstractions of ideas about human nature, as interesting and compelling as they may be. It can only be addressed as it was by those who are part of our spiritual lineage from Abraham to

1

Martin Buber, from the Apostle Paul to Saint Gregory Palamas, through taking our experience seriously and walking the pathways to "purification of the conscience, illumination of the inner person and glorification of the whole person."

The key for many of my secular friends to understanding this pathway has been the clarification of our thinking around "value" and "virtue." *Arete*, virtue, for the ancients including the Church Fathers who lived in and through the Greek language, carries within it the sense of our longing and quest for excellence and our in-born righteousness (Heb. *tsedeq* and *tsedaqah*, "justice" implying a *restoration*). For the ancients sharpness was the *arete* of a knife and strength the *arete* of the boxer. For the Church Fathers compassion was the *arete* of human nature. We were created to be in love. We come to know ourselves in love and we come to know the world, with ourselves in it but not at the centre of it, in cosuffering love. This is the personal experience of the communion the Church articulates in its teaching on the Trinity: the divine communion that is at once creative, incarnate and the "Life of life."

But often through what we perceive as the inadequacy, disappointment or failures of our life we construct an image of ourselves to compensate for our sense of loss. When we misunderstand our struggles, our passions, our self-knowing is changed, and with it our image of all creation. We answer Socrates' call to

2

"know thyself" with an image of our self transplanted onto the thin ground of nostalgia or utopian dreaming. Tragically such infatuations with loss can last a lifetime and provide the seed-bed for whole civilizations. This is the existential source of many cultural and personal ideals and moral systems through which we remake our image of creation.

The attempt to diagnose the estrangement from life is the source of much Existential thinking starting with Nietzsche's heroic attempt to write a *Genealogy of Morals*. Archbishop Lazar has given us the ground upon which to consider a genealogy of *arete*, or virtue, that is large enough to contain the genealogy of morals and lead us to the recovery of our nature and of an understanding of our nature. Those who understand this book will boldly claim Socrates as their teacher because of his fundamental challenge, "Know thyself." Bolder still they will aspire to be disciples of Christ and answer the modern preoccupation with authenticity through cosuffering love and spiritual friendship in each existential encounter.

I
WITH PURPOSE
AND MEANING
A Definition and Discussion
of the Essential Aspects of Existential
Theology

Orthodox Christian theology is, by its very nature, existential. "Existential" is not an arcane philosophy, rather it is a system that encounters the realities of human existence rather than in abstract concepts about humanity and these realities. It speaks in a mode that impacts on and informs the daily struggle of mankind. Orthodox Christian theology does not impute to one guilt for the sins of someone else (the doctrine of "original sin") does not impute any personal guilt for the sacrifice of Christ or deprive people of the freedom of existential responsibility.

It is precisely in this existential aspect that we discover the nature of man and the meaning of our "personhood." Existential theology, like existential philosophy, advocates for an authenticity of life and the personal freedom to take responsibility for shaping the course and quality of meaning in his or her own life. This places a tension between the essence of man– that is, the human nature itself, and the particular essence (hypostasis) of the individual. This is a tension which the theology of the Orthodox Church encounters and offers resolutions to.

Let us make it clear at the outset that we are not entering into the error of "personalism" that has been such a trap for many theologians and writers in the Orthodox Church in the century just past and in our present century. We will explain later why the translation of the patristic expression "*hypostasis*" into "person" has generated misunderstandings.

Among the great existential theologians of the Orthodox Church, few stand out so dramatically as do Saint Gregory Palamas, Saint Symeon the New Theologian and Metropolitan Antony Khrapovitsky. Yet all the Orthodox Church fathers are existentialists because ultimately, there is no other way to approach the Gospel, the life of the Church in this world and the revelation which has been given to us.

Orthodox Christian existential theology stands in opposition to the dry, legalistic moral fascism of Western scholastic theology.

Scholasticism is concerned with attempts at minute philosophical and legalistic definitions of the very mysteries of human existence. It is concerned with abstractions removed from actual human experience.

One of the problems with the scholastics was (and still is), according to Canadian philosopher David J. Goa, that they tend to substitute the truth with the "wording" or "phrasing" of the truth. There is a kind of linguistic positivism in scholastic formulations. It is as if they believe that language as a tool can actually produce "truth." However, language obviously can only "signify" the truth. By missing the difference scholasticism became trapped in reflective analysis and in a literal understanding of "authentic" sources.

Attempting to find the truth of life in formulations of any kind results in trapping life in their own inflexible patterns. This is what we often call "ideology" and we must certainly be careful to avoid understanding the faith in such a manner. The antidote to this mistake cannot be subjective individual experience, obtained in a private manner.

SEEKING COHERENCE

Even faith, individual and private, can be a false guide. On this ground, one may raise an objection to experience-as-knowledge attained by individual "meditation." However, in the Church we are not alone and we are never isolated individuals. We are "in communion" with one another and with the saints, and with Christ. This "communion," this personal mode of being, can be truly implemented in the Church. The coherence of this experience and its "authenticity" is fine-tuned by the Holy Spirit. This is, moreover, why we always look for the "consensus" of the holy fathers.

This "consensus" is not just a technicality or an agreement in wording or concepts, rather it is directly related to the "coherence" brought about by the Spirit. In this sense, "coherence" can be another way of saying experience-as-knowledge. This does not mean that all individual experience, particularly the experiences encountered by studying nature or meditating upon natural things in faith, is wrong or misleading. Such experiences very often make sense and can help people in their spiritual journey.

God has not left us helpless and without some guidance. We all have a compass — the image of God imprinted on our soul. I think this is what is meant by Apostle Paul when he says that those who do not know the law do according to the law by their own nature. (The law here is knowledge of the truth).

The fulfilment of knowledge and coherent experience of the faith can, however, only be trustworthily known in the Church, where Christ is not simply reflected (as through in a mirror) but is present in person.

Existentialism is a practical approach to both theology and philosophy. It is not concerned with abstractions which do not relate to actual human experience; rather, as indicated above, it impacts the concrete realities of human experience and the human struggle. Existentialism is concerned with the reality and meaning of human existence, the relationship of the human person to other human beings and to the universe. Christian and Jewish existentialists have also been deeply concerned with man's relationship with God. For Orthodox Christian theology, this relationship is the very centre of "experience."

For many, those dogmatic expressions of faith such as the concept of the Holy Trinity, of divine grace, the work of the Holy Spirit and the Incarnation, may appear, on the surface, to be remote from the lives and struggles of humanity. As St Antony (Khrapovitsky) has demonstrated so clearly, however, these dogmas of the faith interject into our lives and form the very foundation of our moral struggle in this life.[1]

For convenience, I have chosen to refer to "negative" and "positive" existentialism. This is not a

8

"values judgment" or a ranking of the two schools. By "negative," I mean those philosophers who believe that man's place in the universe is essentially meaningless while the "positive" school sees man as having place and meaning in the universe. The Christian existentialists see this meaning through our relationship with God.

ISLAND OR PENNENSULA?
"SELF" IN A SEA OF "OTHERS"

There is no other point that we can start from, no questions we can ask, no knowledge we can seek without an awareness of our own personal existence. As human beings, we are compelled by our nature to be cognizant of ourselves as the first thing in our experience that "exists" in any meaningful way. Our own vector to meaning is our subjective awareness of our own existence in relation to the things we may know, be aware of, or ascribe meaning to. We see ourselves from the inside. Our vision orients us to the outside world and makes sense of it by relating it to our *self*, and our *self* to it. For us, the world is identified by our own existence in it, and its primary meaning is that it is the place in which we exist. All other meaning and awareness arises from and expands outward from this fundamental sense of reality. It may be that even our development of self-awareness in infancy arises from our cognition of "the other," the "not I" in relation to the "I." While this is an essential point of departure, existentialism is very much concerned with our turning away from self-centredness and opening ourselves toward the fact that to live is to be related to others. Paradoxically, we must do this without losing the sense of our subjective self, of our complete subjective freedom. All of our learning and human growth begins with an awareness of "self," and we begin to learn and understand by relating the things we perceive to ourselves and ourselves to them. In this instance, an existentialist "breakthrough" occurs when we understand that others are necessary for the understanding of our own "self," and hopefully apply Kant's imperative that we treat others as ends in themselves and not as a means only — a thought derived from the almost universal "Golden Rule." This aspect of existentialism figures very much in the thought of Christian and Jewish philosophers such as Kierkegaard, Buber, Marcel,[2] and Dostoevsky,[3] and even in the works of the atheist Heidegger. Negative existentialists such as Sartre,[4] on the other hand, see the self in opposition to others (hence his aphorism, "hell is other people"). We might also use the appellation "negative" because of the negation of objective, fact-based values advocated by Sartre and others. Sartre, like his Positivist counter-parts such as Bertrand Russell,[5] would arrive at a subjective relativism concerning values, morals and ethics, "right and wrong," though by a rather different route than the Positivists.

Russell, for example, arrives at relativism by asserting that only science can give us *real* answers while Sartre would argue subjective relativism on the basis of human freedom. Moral absolutism is just as dangerous to society as moral relativism. Part of the reason for the collapse of Christianity as a viable moral force in a modern, pluralistic environment has been the expectation that it produced immutable absolutes in the realms of values and ethics, where both science and valid experience would show that it did not. Such "absolutism" was forced upon Christianity from the human level. At best, these absolutes were arrived at from an egoistic point of view, at worst, by the legalistic interpretations of crude fundamentalism which knew little of the truth of human nature and the essence of a humanity it claimed to govern. Some of these moral absolutisms actually formed a hindrance to salvation, and when they were proved in error, (and were always in error when they were used as an excuse to kill people) many people began to lose faith. As Nikolai Berdyaev points out, when Christianity is corrupted into an ideology then, like any ideology,[6] it can be turned to the service of egoism. Kierkegaard and Shestov,[7] from the Existentialist side, would argue in favour of universal obligations and against personalistic relativism. At the end of his *Athens and Jerusalem*, he asserts that "Philosophy is not a mulling over, but a struggle. And this struggle is

11

endless and will never end. The Kingdom of God, as it is written, is attained through violence." "The opposite of necessity," Shestov declares, "is possibility."

When Christianity is turned into an ideology, which it most certainly has been by the "religious right," then none of its "absolutes" can be trusted. Only when it remains an ontological process is it authentic Christianity — a vehicle for our transformation from purification to illumination to glorification — the path to *theosis*. We cannot be saved by a legislated moral code or set of values, but only by the struggle for *theosis* in the Holy Spirit. At best, a code can be a guideline, but a moral code so easily becomes a substitute for a life in Christ that it can be idolatrous, especially when it is proclaimed to be "absolute."

The expectation of "absolutes" in this life is an invitation to demagogues and dictators and a recipe for failure. One should not equate "absolutes" with what is necessarily true. "Truth" and "absolute" are not synonyms. "Absolute is more likely to be a synonym for "ossified mind," "ignorance," or autocracy.

It is a paradox of existentialism (though not unique to it) that the concepts of this philosophy may be used as an instrument in the quest for meaning, or as a negation of the idea of meaning. Our existence might ultimately be a meaningless accident in a universe which we happen to infest, rather than a universe that is purposely habitable by us. However, even with the concept of an accidentally occurring universe with a randomly mechanical process of evolution, such an idea is untenable. If the universe evolved accidentally, we would nevertheless be an integral part of the same process that brought the universe into being, and even a result of it, and so it would still be a meaningful place of our existence, intimately related to our own being.

Since we believe that the universe, evolutionary or not, is the wilful, intentional creation of God, and that man is the apex of that process, we will assert, no differently, that our existence and the processes of the universe as a whole are intimately related and have meaning to one another.

The ultimate questions in theology are straightforwardly existential: we exist in time, space and place. What do we do with it? What are we responsible for, what are we not responsible for? How do we conduct our lives and what is the ultimate meaning of our existence? Some existentialists will assert that our existence has no ultimate meaning but that we are nonetheless responsible for shaping the quality and course of our lives.[8]

It is true that life often seems to be a series of absurdities which we respond to with a repertoire of futilities, but this is far from being true. In fact, Orthodox Christian theology will give us a truly meaningful and coherent answer to every one of the

13

existential questions, and will lead us to profoundly understand, or at least grasp, the meaning of existence.

PART AND WHOLE:
NATURE AND PERSONHOOD
Existence and Essence

The perplexing question posed in philosophy concerning essence and existence needs to be addressed as we begin our discussion. First of all, the definition or meaning of the term "essence" is understood in different ways at different times by different philosophers. To make the question more complex still, there is the question of the differentiation between the general essence of mankind, and the particular essence of a given individual.

In philosophy in general, essence is abstract while "existence" is more concrete. However, in Orthodox Christian thought we use the term essence in a concrete way. With regard to man, essence signifies what is common to all and subject to the laws of nature.

This difference should alert us to the difficulties we are about to encounter in expressing the historical sense of such ontological categories in Orthodox theology using today's philosophical language. Nevertheless, we shall make our best attempt at it, offering the statement just made as a caveat.

Let us say at the beginning that we will not be able to adequately express the difference between the general essence of man and particular essence of an individual person without introducing the patristic ontological category of *hypostasis*. There could be no freedom without *self*. There must be a personhood capable of self determination, for only in this way can we distinguish a free action from a mechanical reaction. We denote this personhood as *hypostasis* and throughout this work, *hypostasis* is used to indicate the particular essence of the individual person for reasons we will discuss later. "Person," even "personhood" is not adequate to express the concept of a "particular essence." The philosophy of "Personalism" will not do.

The apparently opposing suppositions that "essence precedes existence" or that "existence precedes essence"[9] are both pregnant with meaning and ripe for misunderstanding. While the question is certainly ontological, we will assert that it primarily sets in logical order the basis of knowing.

Let me say at the outset that the question of "essence" is confusing, partly because essentialism itself is, to a certain degree, questionable. From a purely Orthodox Christian point of view, essentialism is problematic because the applications of the concept often confuse the difference we make between essence and *energy* in both our understanding of God and in our anthropology. As we mentioned, the essence of

15

humanity (that which all have in common — our nature) and the particular essence of the individual person (*hypostasis*) are both necessary to our understanding of Orthodox theology.

THE WEAKNESS OF ESSENTIALISM

To the degree essentialism may have validity,[10] we would reject the Platonistic concept (to know the essence of something is to know the ultimate truth of its being because essence is an immutable archetypal form)[11] or the Aristotelian idea (to know the essence of something is to know its true definition or nomenclature).[12] We cannot entertain the extreme view of Leibnitz that there can be only one ultimate reason why a thing exists: its essence demands that it exist, and it will, therefore, ultimately exist unless its existence is superseded by the similar demand on the part of another essence.[13] We will also disregard Locke's notions (expressed in his third essay). From an Orthodox Christian point of view, the essence of mankind would be the common human nature which God created, which fell, and which Christ assumed in order to redeem it by restoring it (recapitulation) and bringing it back into communion with God, bringing those who will to *theosis*. We have discussed this in an appendix to the book.

ESSENCE AND THE INDIVIDUAL

16

We are human because we are of that human nature. If the human nature was not single, that is, if there was not but one nature of all mankind which all humanity has in common and is shared by all, then we would have to understand human nature, not as an actual essence, but as an abstract concept. Not only would this have no existential dimension, but it could not provide any basis for conceiving that redeeming grace sanctified the human nature, and not the human individual as an isolated entity.

It is precisely because this concept of the human nature as an actual essence was lost in the West that the doctrine of "Original Sin" could take root. If the human nature was not an actual essence, shared in common by all humanity, then it would be necessary to explain the problem of the Ancestral Sin exclusively by means of hereditary rights and hereditary vengeance. We could not say that the "essence" which all have in common is wounded or fallen, but that each individual inherits personally this "hereditary guilt" (much as the offspring of families inherit an on-going vendetta). This concept, like the Western dogma of "Atonement" requires the construction of a labyrinthine legal fiction which leaves little freedom to the individual and little space for a free individual personhood. This is just what Augustine and the later Medieval Latin theologians did. They could not even justify the idea of a *generic guilt*, but only of an hereditary one. This was one of the most critical errors of Western philosophical theology. It also produced a concept of a tyrannical and supremely unjust God.

Let us, for the moment, examine an apparent contradiction. If we speak of the "essence of humanity" as an abstraction in which the individual has no personal freedom, no authentic, independent personhood, we would have an abstract idea with no existential content. The essence can be known only in individual persons. In patristic literature, we find the expressed idea that, *en tois prosopois i ousia* "the essence can only be found in persons." The nature which we can know in humanity is one because it is common to all, but we know it only in individuals. This is evident to us in that Christ could assume this essence in its wholeness in His own Person. We therefore can speak of essence only in the context of what is truly common in man, not what one becomes or forms from his own qualities, the personal freedom of each human hypostasis.

Clearly, we need yet another ontological category in order to properly express our Orthodox Christian understanding as against the essentialist concept. That second ontological category is *hypostasis*. It is *hypostasis* that relates to what I might become and includes my personal differentiation and particularity. We might refer to it as our "particular essence" as opposed to the common or general essence of mankind — our common human nature. If our differentiation and particularity were encapsuled in the common human essence, then we would need only one ontological category to interpret logical existence: the category of an expanded and dynamical essence that includes our personal destination also. Philosophically, such an idea is consistent and harmonizes with the philosophical tradition (essentialism) which holds essence to signify all the attributes of existence, but it could have no real existential dimension.

We utilize two ontological categories, therefore, to interpret logical existence. The first is our nature or "essence," which refers to a down-to-earth, biological entity which is inherited and transmitted. Our *hypostasis*, on the other hand, signifies our personal differentiation, our freedom from nature, or perhaps our freedom to rise above "nature." This is something which is not a property of human nature, though it is present to all sentient beings. This is a mystery of grace, a "mode" of existence which is given to our nature. This existential "mode" is the logical aspect of our essence which, while affected by the common human nature, is not comprised of it but is given externally by the grace of God.

In the sense of essence as the common human nature, the essence certainly precedes our individual existence, but not the existence of humanity since both the essence and existence began at the same moment.[14] Existence is necessary in order to know that there is an essence and to have an idea what the essence is, so in the order of knowledge (not being), existence precedes essence. In this sense, it is a question of cognizance, not theoretical metaphysics.[15] From an Orthodox Christian point of view, this approach simply states that we come to know God in relation to our own being, our own awareness of our existence in the universe.

Perhaps, however, we should go a bit further with this question and add a few other concepts. We might suggest that from a more purely philosophical point of view, we could assert that one forms one's own essence. In that case, our essence would be what we do with our existence: thus, I make myself a farmer or a teacher — my essence. Seen in this light, one could suggest that the stuff (my intelligence, my will, my substance) out of which I make my essential self must precede my essence. Following this concept, what I will become is my essence, how I will become that relates to my energies. My "*Energy*" is how and what I do with the "stuff" out of which I make my essential self.[16] In this regard, we may say that "sin" is best defined as the misuse of our energies.

There is a certain truth in that basic concept, but we would not completely agree. We would have to say that what each individual makes of himself relates to his *hypostasis*, not his essence. Why is this difference important? For one thing, what we do with the "stuff" out of which "I" make my self- identity or quality is not common to all humanity. Essence, however, is that which is common to all. What I do with the stuff out of which I make my essential self is individual; it relates to my *hypostasis*, not to that common human nature. Christ has redeemed our nature by recapitulating human nature in Himself, and He offers us by grace a new nature, a new essence (Eph.4:23-24; Col.3:10).[17] If our future can in any way be our essence, then that future is to become divine, which all those who attain it will have in common. Theosis is the destination to which we have been called, for: "Whereby are given unto us exceeding great and precious promises: that by these ye might be partakers of the divine nature...*(2 Peter 1:4)*.

I might prefer to leave matters at this level, but the complex question of essence is central in nature and cannot be left unaddressed. Moreover it has dimensions. We do not speak of the Essence of God in the same frame that we speak of the created essence of man, and even when we speak of the essence of the Church, we are not speaking in the same context as when we speak of the essence of man. Indeed, we will have to speak about the essence of the Church in some detail in order to more fully grasp the concepts we are speaking of.

In purely philosophical terms, such distinctions rarely (if ever) appear, but in terms of Orthodox Christian ontology and theology, they are of great significance. The question of precedence of existence and essence in order of *being* must be touched upon. It is my own view that, unless we reduce mind and spirit to a complex of electro-chemical reactions and processes, we simply cannot know essence in the realm of being. We can know *of* the essence of humanity, and we can know some things about it, but we cannot *know* it. We will not turn away from the idea of a transformation or transfiguration by grace, which is a restoration rather than a "becoming." If our essence is what we are in common, our nature, it may also be what we (mankind) can be restored to by grace. In fact, the most meaningful expression we might give to the question is from the ontological point of view of cause and priority in the plan of God for humanity in common, even though not everyone will choose to become that and participate in the restored and sanctified human nature. If our essence is that which we as humanity have in common, that is the human nature (in our understanding, a fallen nature), then we can grasp the idea that, if our unique ancestors ended up with a fallen nature, that is what their descendants would all share in common. Not guilt or even responsibility. Responsibility must then be assigned to our *hypostasis*, what we ourselves do with that freedom of personhood. Christ has redeemed it by recapitulating this human nature in Himself, and He offers us by grace a new nature, a new essence (Eph.4:23-24; Col.3:10).[18] If our future can in any way be our essence, then that future is to become divine, which all those who attain it will have in common. One might say then that our essence is what all humanity now has

22

in common, but in future, we may receive by divine grace that new nature which the community of the redeemed will all have in common.[19] The Church as the Body of Christ is the unifying projection of the recapitulated nature redeemed by Christ Jesus. It is the matrix of our *theosis* because it is the projection of the divinized human nature of Christ, a fully human nature seated at the right hand of the Glory, fully united with the divine in and by Christ Jesus.

We are, after all, not immortal by nature. We receive immortality as a gift of divine grace and what is received by grace is exterior to our nature; it cannot be "owned" by, or integral to, our nature or essence. Our divinization will also be a gift of grace, an indwelling of the *Energy* of God and in that sense we also cannot refer to it as our essence in any ordinary understanding of the word, even though in the following paragraphs we will use the term. It should be read in the context of transfiguration.

We cannot move on without stipulating that the meaning of the "fallen nature" is essentially a proclivity to habitually misuse our energies. It is not some pan-human substratum or "entity" which has become totally depraved or evil. Man should have fulfilled a vocation as a unifying element in nature, for he is not only its crown, but the microcosm of creation, possessing within himself both its spiritual and physical dimensions. This vocation could only have been fulfilled through unselfish love and the absence of egotism. This would have constituted a proper use of his energies. The fall really constitutes this proclivity to habitually misuse our energies, *not the loss of them.*

Christ healed this misuse through His perfect humanity, in Whom the perfect human nature is expressed, making unity with God and the cosmos again possible for human beings — a unity which Christ realized for us in His unity of perfect humanity with complete divinity. Human nature, restored in Him, has now the ability to make the proper use of its energies. This proper use is manifested in the Church, His Body, even if the members of the Church so often fall short of it. As we mentioned, the Church is the matrix on which we work this out with the help of grace.

The principle of deification *(theosis)* is planted in each one of us at baptism; that principle is the Holy Spirit. This is the often overlooked meaning of being "regenerated (born again) by water and the spirit". It follows that our life in Christ is the process of deification, or the gradual acquisition of the Holy Spirit, but this relates to our *hypostasis*, not our essence. Here, we might suggest, is the very heart of Orthodox Christian existentialism: the process of sanctification, of perfec-tionment, and glorification, "to partake of the divine nature" (2Pt.1:4), which in a sense we already have, for example in the Holy Eucharist. We could not become divine (our destination essence —

rather, the intended destination of the common human nature) if the Divine did not already exist. It is not our essence until we become that by grace, even though we, in a manner of speaking, *hypostatically* already partake of it before we become what will be our glorified essence. We become that not without applying our *Energy*, and when we acquire it, it is the *Energy* of God that fills our existence. We may know *of* that essence, but we cannot *know* it until we experience it, which not everyone will.

The very fact that, in the end, not everyone will share in that essence, which will be the common nature of redeemed humanity, reminds us that the concept of *hypostasis* is vital. Christ redeemed the fallen human nature, but we become participants in that redemption *hypostatically* — that is, as individual, differentiated persons. As the common human nature is known in each person, the redemption of that nature is manifested in each person who chooses it and struggles for it. Since we are speaking about a "nature" or "essence," we will understand that choosing redemption makes us part of a community in which all will have the new nature in common. This in itself is part of the mystery of the Holy Church as the body of Christ. Without this necessity of community, a radical individualism would lead us back into the bondage of a self-absorbed egotism.

If we were bound by a universal nature or essence subject to the laws of nature and had this only, then we might be bound irrevocably to the whole with little freedom. We might be bound to instinctive or automatic behaviour, even while our intellect carried our social structures forward. Since, as we have discussed, we also have that particular essence which we call *hypostasis*, we also have moral freedom and a free will to act in ways which contradict or even oppose the common human nature, our essence. We have the capacity of real responsibility and ascent.

ENDNOTES:

[1]. See his *The Moral Idea of the Main Dogmas of the Faith*, (Synaxis Press, Dewdney, B.C., 2001).

[2]. Soren Aabye Kierkegaard (1813-1855) Danish philosopher often credited as the father of modern existentialism. He was deeply pious and sought to bring Lutherans into a more active relationship with Christ and practice of their religion. Gabriel Marcel (1889-1973) French philosopher and devoutly Roman Catholic existentialist. Martin Buber (1878-1965) Austrian born existentialist philosopher, Buber was a devout Jew. He applied existentialist principles to his interpretation of the Hebrew Scripture (the "Old Testament").

[3]. Fyodor (Theodore) Dostoevsky (1821-1881) One of Russia's most famous authors, Dostoevsky actually contributed more than many other existentialist, as he gave us a "world of existentialism" in his array of novels and stories. His work is laced with many profoundly Orthodox Christian theological precepts.

[4]. Jean Paul Sartre (1905-1980). French atheist existentialist philosopher of what we have termed the "negative school."

[5]. Lord Bertrand A.W. Russell (3rd Earl Russell) (1872-1970) English Mathematician and Positivist philosopher. His view of ethics may be termed subjective relativism.

[6]. In *Freedom and Slavery*.

[7]. Lev Shestov (1866-1938). Russian existentialist philosopher and prolific writer. In the midst of his philosophy, we also find this confession of faith: "Faith, only the faith that looks to the Creator and that He inspires, radiates

from itself the supreme and decisive truths condemning what is and what is not. Reality is transfigured. The heavens glorify the Lord. The prophets and apostles cry in ecstasy, "O death, where is thy sting? Hell, where is thy victory?" And all announce: "Eye hath not seen, nor ear heard, neither have entered into the heart of man, the things which God hath prepared for them that love Him." (Cp. 1Cor.15:55, 2:9)

[8]. This is an assertion of free will by both religious and non-religious existential philosophers, which accords well with Orthodox concepts. Among both the deeply religious and the atheist existentialists, personal responsibility and the discovery of meaning for one's own life are of signal importance. Those like Sartre may have felt that life was meaning-less, and perhaps his was. However, the equally atheistic Albert Camus places the discovery of the meaning of one's life at the very centre of such novels as *The Plague*, where it is the inescapable tragedy that finally develops meaning in the lives of the protagonists, even providing a better and more noble death to some who had previously been leading meaningless lives. In *L'Etranger*, the protagonists Meursault, finds meaning only on his way to the gallows. He is suddenly filled with an exhilaration, because his death sentence is the only occasion on which he must finally take responsibility for anything in his life.

On the other hand, in *The Trial*, Kafka gives us Iosef K, who is his own prison and his own accuser. This is why the priest in the cathedral, where K finds himself alone, announces that he is the "prison chaplain." The "trial" is taking place within K's own mind, his psyche, his subconscious. He never discovers what the charges against him are, and never resolves them. In the end, he "executes" himself in a quarry on the edge of the city. He never realised any meaning to his life and could not take responsibility for his own actions and decisions. This is why he is depicted as never reaching the court and never discovering what he has been charged with. In *Metamorphosis*, Gregor rather likes being a huge insect because, in that condition, he is not so obliged to take responsibility for his life, and his life can be rather blissfully meaningless.

Dostoevsky, who gives us a world of existentialism, is a deeply devout Orthodox Christian. He gives the profound dimension to the existentialism that we identify with Orthodox theology. "One Christian is no Christian," the desert fathers say. We come to know ourselves only through our relationships with other people. Let us take the two essentially meaningless lives in *Crime and Punishment* for example. Rodion Raskolnikov and Arkady Svidrigailov are both "outsiders" who are lost in their own personal meaninglessness and emptiness. The final redemption of Raskolnikov is mediated by the totally unselfish, compassionate love of Sofia (Sonia). At one critical point, Svidrigailov seeks this kind of redemption from Darya, but she is unable to provide it. Svidrigailov, decides that the meaninglessness of his life is final, and commits suicide. Dostoevsky here intends to demonstrate the Orthodox Christian concept of the power of cosuffering love to serve for the spiritual healing of the one whose life appears to be without meaning and without hope. Orthodox Christian existential theology leads toward both ultimate meaning and transformation.

[9]. I believe that in our time, this was primarily Jean Paul Sartre's question and he advocated that existence precedes essence. In fact, he would say, we exist and create our own essence. We would not radically disagree with him in that, but would have quite different ideas about how our Energy is employed in this and what the ultimate destination of this "essence creating" is. We would argue that it is our *hypostasis* rather than our essence that gives us moral freedom. We will touch on these matters as we go. (Energy here is used in the Orthodox theological context).

[10]. Let me note that one advance in essentialism has appeared, first in the feminist movement and later, during the 1990s in several studies and a number of popular books. This advance has been the realization of the asymmetry between the sexuality and mode of communication in males and females. This is something that was obfuscated by the Behaviourists and denied in the early feminist movement, where it was supposed that sexuality, or differences in sexuality, was learned behaviour which could be changed by changing the early teaching environment. The tragic bankruptcy of Behavioursim is now known and the fact that essential asymmetries between male and female are in the general essence of gender, not in programming. Sexual identity is in the brain; it is present at birth. This is why, sometimes, the brain and the genitalia are not for the same sex.

[11]. We should explain this a bit further, but in order to avoid an exceptionally lengthy footnote, I have placed this discussion as Appendix I at the end of this text. The Appendix is titled, PLATONISTIC ESSENTIALISM.

[12]. When Aristotle speaks of *formal cause* he is not indicating abstract forms but is speaking of the meaning or purpose of a thing.

[13]. *Filosoph. Schriften*. VII. 3-3, 3-5, 3-10.

[14]. "Adam" signifies "first man" and "Eve" signifies "first woman." Both were created — came into existence — as humans with a common essence that signifies "humanity." Both were also created as individuals, that is as "hypostases." They became the fountainhead of the common human nature, but not of "*hypostasis*."

[15]. We should say something about the term *metaphysics* because it has more than one meaning. Apparently, the term was invented inadvertently when collators of Aristotle's work placed his writing on *Wisdom* just after his book titled *Physics*. The book on wisdom was given the descriptive name *meta-physics*, meaning "after the *Physics*." Metaphysics took on the idea of that which is beyond physics or beyond the physical and it is generally understood in an esoteric manner with connotations such as spiritual, abstract, an unseen or invisible reality, etc. It also often has the connotation of that which concerns higher existence or higher being or some kind of superphysical ontology. We will accord it all these meanings in this work.

[16]. We are using "energy" and "energies" in the mode of Orthodox theology or ontology. If, as Christians, our *essence* is what we are to be in the Holy Spirit, our *energy* is our logical choices, obedience to God, spiritual orientation, etc. Orthodox theology makes a difference between essence and energy. The energy and grace of God are uncreated, everything about man is created.

[17]. *And be renewed in the spirit of your mind; And that ye put on the new man, which after God is created in righteousness and true holiness (Eph.4:23-24). And have put on the new man, which is renewed in knowledge after the image of him that created him. (Colossians 3:10)*

[18]. *And be renewed in the spirit of your mind; And that ye put on the new man, which after God is created in righteousness and true holiness (Eph.4:23-24). And have put on the new man, which is renewed in knowledge after the image of him that created him. (Colossians 3:10)*

[19]. On the other hand, the essence of the Church is what she will become, that is, the Kingdom of God. She is even now becoming what she will be. She is, in a sense, the Kingdom; but of course, her end is predetermined by God. So in this sense, the essence precedes her existence (at least in the will of God). This may recall Aristotle's proposition that the oak tree (the essence) is already present in the acorn (existence). Scripture tells us that the tree was created and given the power to produce the acorn. Nevertheless, the essence of the Church as Kingdom of God is logically anterior but existentially posterior. The essence of mankind must always be regarded differently than the essence of anything else.

29

II
THEOLOGY OF LIFE
A Concept of Orthodox
Christian Existential Theology

"Energy" is about relationships, whether it is the created Energy of the universe or the Energy of man, or the uncreated Energy of God. All things exist only in relation to other things and we can truly know ourselves only in relation to others and to God.

A common dictionary definition of "existentialism" reduces it to those particular existentialist doctrines that deny objective universal values and hold that each person must create values for himself through his own experience of life, in such a way that he lives each moment to the full. In reality, existentialism may recognize that such objective moral value exists and acknowledge, as we must, that competing systems make the claim to represent them. In this regard, what existentialism advocates is that we either make a free moral choice among them, or freely reject them.

A system may be said to be existential when it actually helps, in a creative and supportive way, to shape and form our values and concept of life, and what we become. A theological system can be said to be existential when its doctrines and precepts can not only be experienced, but also be verified by experience, and when it is itself a dynamic, living encounter which can be verified both by the experience of its present adherents and the lives of those who have gone before.

We have offered a general definition of existentialism in the first chapter of this book, but it is necessary to explain what I mean when I refer to Orthodox theology and teachings as "existential." First, allow me to state the premises upon which I base the observation, and then I will discuss some concrete examples. Remember that existentialism is as much concerned with freedom of the will and responsibility as it is with any other aspects of life. It is also very much concerned with the meaning of our free choices and the meaning of human existence itself. Being existential, such theology also cannot be ossified and unable to respond gracefully to new knowledge in an open and creative way. After all, only that which responds in terms of the *realities of human existence* is called "existential."

I would like to give the framework of existentialism within which I am speaking and indicate the existentialist grid through which Orthodox Christian teaching and theology may be viewed. It is my contention that all truly Orthodox theology is essentially and profoundly existential and that scholasticism and all forms of Augustinianism create a break, usually radical, in the flow of that Orthodox

31

Christian theological process which renders it effective in actually shaping and forming, in our daily lives, who we are and what we are to become. Here are the three touchstones upon which I base this view of our theology. An existentialist approach to theology begins with the premises that dogma, doctrine, every aspect of theology and Orthodox Christian teaching must:

1. speak in a clear, coherent way to the nature of human *existence* — that is, the essence of our being as humans — and it must do so not in the coy, dry, moralistic way that scholastic thought does, but in a vital way that impacts on our actual lives and beings. It must give meaning to our existence in a believable and vital way that shuns such rather empty slogans as "man was created for worship," or more empty still, "this life is simply a testing ground in which we prepare for the next life."

2. deal with the primary dimension of the meaning of existence (rather than, for example, regulatory precepts of human behaviour or legalistic strictures on the manifestations of human will and actions).

3. present the *means* of arriving at concrete meaning in personal existence, rather than the dogmatization of abstract legalistic definitions of "the norm," or categories of behaviour.

As a fourth stipulation, I place the clearly

existentialist requirement of St Antony Khrapovitsky, Metropolitan of Kiev, that all Orthodox Christian dogma must be not a mere legislated and obligatory doctrine, but rather it must be manifested as a revelation which serves as an underpinning for our daily moral lives. Dogma is essentially something that must be *experienced* in the process of life itself, rather than simply obeyed. The holy fathers did not elucidate the dogmas of Christ by means of a philosophical dialectic or by reflective reasoning on some premise given symbolically or "in seed form" to be developed later by rationalization. They comprehended the dogmas of Christ by means of a living experience in a life deeply surrendered to Christ.[1] We call this revelation "theoria." Al-though this is a word borrowed from Hellenic philosophy, and generally indicating a deep contemplation, we add the concept of *"revelation"* to it. Therefore dogma is revealed through the Holy Spirit to those great theologians who have given themselves over to a deep, prayerful contemplation, in a life in Christ. The very comprehension of dogma is an existential process which we call *theoria*. There is no "new" dogma, nor "dogmatic development," as the delusion *(plani; prelest)* of Sectarians would have us believe,[2] rather there is a coming into accord with and thus a comprehension of and ability to express in unchanging modes, the revealed and ever-present dogmas of Christ. This is an existential process involving our own transformation, never a process of developing dogmas, and never a process that takes place by rationalization or reflective reasoning. It is a process of life itself. We are shaped and formed, and find the fulness of meaning in the divine dogmas and the living theology of Orthodoxy. It is a paradox that we discover this fulness by participating in it, and we receive it only in the process of experiencing it. This is the mystery of the indwelling of the Holy Spirit.

Above all else, existentialism is the quest for "meaning," and even those existentialist philosophers who sought to negate any real meaning at least had to come to grips with the *concept* of "meaning."

It is necessary to follow these prefatory remarks with some clear examples of the existential nature of both Orthodox Christian theology and the general Orthodox way of life. Since the principles of asceticism are fundamental to Orthodox Christian theology, we will examine the existentialist dimension of that asceticism which is appropriate to the normal flow of Orthodox Christian daily life. We need take only one or two examples in order to make this more clear.

Unfortunately, most people think of asceticism only in terms of some kind of heavy repression, an almost neurotic disdain for one's humanity, or a Gnostic hatred of the body. This is sad because asceticism is then viewed as something completely negative, as something that can have nothing to do with our real lives — something that could never have a truly existential dimension. We think of asceticism as practically an aberration (even if a holy and positive one) that is only for monastics who go into the desert and live in caves, and we forget that asceticism is a normal and presupposed part of the Orthodox Christian life, something expected to be commonplace for all believing Orthodox Christians. Asceticism means "training." This is both its primary meaning and its purpose in our Christian lives.

Locked into the misconception that asceticism means repression, very few people understand it as a vital and even joyous means of spiritual growth and development, an adventure in discovery that opens to us the fulness of our humanity and personhood *(hypostasis)* even while it helps to elevate us above the limitations of human nature. It is something very positive.[3] The truth is that everything we do, no matter how simple, to train ourselves for a truly Christian life, is asceticism. Avoiding the ascetic aspect of Christian life demonstrates a lack of understanding of the nature of the Church as the body of Christ.

We may not think about the regular fasts as asceticism, but when we discuss aspects of the fast other than restrictions from certain foods, the matter becomes more clear. If we speak about fasting with the eyes and with the tongue in addition to the food restrictions, we begin to think more about spiritual struggle and asceticism.

Since people are used to thinking about asceticism in negative terms, most of the time when we talk about, for example, asceticism of the eye, the listener will think in terms of avoidance. We quickly moralize the concept and think it means to avoid gazing or even looking at things or people which cause us to have sinful thoughts. The same pertains to asceticism of the tongue; we also think of *avoidance*. The greatest part of the asceticism of the eye, however, is to train ourselves for *the encounter.*

Not too many decades ago, even in public schools, the idea of training the eye was part of the curriculum. Art appreciation classes were understood as a necessary part of training a young person, because it was known that the eye had to be trained for discernment. In the coarse, materialistic days of the 1950's and early 1960's, art and music appreciation classes began to be viewed as "unnecessary frills." They did nothing to enhance one's economic prospects, so they were a "waste of time and money."

One of the reasons some people do not like correct and strict icons is because their eyes have not been trained. Not only do they not have spiritual discernment, but they do not even have the means of making careful aesthetic judgments. Their eye has not been trained for discernment in an Orthodox way; they have not practised the asceticism of the eye. For the untrained eye (which sees things in a worldly way) Western style humanistic paintings may seem more appealing, largely because they convey no spiritual discernment, no understanding of purification and transfiguration. Even when the untrained eye decides that it likes Orthodox Christian icons, it is often from a New Age spiritualistic perspective: the icon appears to be something spiritual in the New Age sense of the word, and it has become used in this pantheistic manner.[4]

This is why we have so many ill prepared icon painters in North America today, and such corrupt examples in Russia and Greece.. Iconography has been preempted by the New Age Movement,[5] with frequent pantheistic and humanistic distortions. Often, we see icons being painted with naturalistic landscapes backing figures painted with Hari Krishna colours and pietistic countenances. They are seen as "spiritual," but are totally lacking in any Orthodox Christian theological content, without any real idea of transfiguration and glorification or valid concept of *theosis*. Many people who lack discernment or who are penetrated with New Age delusion like Byzantine icons because they see something mystical in them, whereas the icon speaks of things that should be commonplace to the believing Orthodox Christian. Because their eyes have never been trained to encounter the icon, they do not understand what it actually means and frequently do not care.[6] Like Protestants with the Scripture, they interpret the icon with subjective emotionalism and disdain the idea that it is not for any personal interpretation, but should be a faithful witness to the Apostolic Tradition. A true icon painter really does have to rise above subjective aesthetics and accept the universal, objective value of the contents of the art.[7]

Asceticism of the eye is a truly existential concept. It goes far beyond providing us with a disciplined discernment of objects. We also have to train our eyes to *encounter each other*. Our gaze can be trained in such a way that it never wounds another person. At a higher level our gaze can be trained in such a way that it serves in the healing process. Many times we can wound other people with our eyes. For example, when we see homeless people who live on the street we encounter them with the eye. Some people think that these street people are all worthless, lazy "bums," and they look upon them with eyes of disdain or even contempt. In fact, almost all these "street people" are there because they have mental illness or severe emotional problems. Even among the teenagers who have run away from home and ended up on the street, there are often serious emotional or mental problems. An untrained eye which has not been formed with the true concepts of Christianity might look upon these people with disgust or with a condescending pity. Such a gaze can deeply wound a person and push them down deeper into their despair and grief. What these people really need from us is a gaze *which validates their humanity* — not a condescending pity, but a look of self-recognition, the exchange of glances between two human beings who recognize their equality. Compassion wears an open and friendly look, not the doleful, condescending eye of pity. An ascetic eye will always look upon them as *fellow* human beings equal in every way to oneself. The truly ascetic eye would not look upon these people with pity, knowing instinctively that to do so would actually wound them more. More than this, the ascetic eye would not even be capable of such a destructive reaction. The ascetic eye can automatically look on these people with a kind of *co-suffering* that will validate their humanity and radiate the love of Christ. It is also a look of self-recognition and understanding this is necessary for the acquisition of cosuffering love.

It is more difficult to lie with our eyes than it is to lie with our tongues. We can say flattering or nice things to another person without any sincerity, but our eyes usually give us away. We can even ask our brother or sister for forgiveness without sincerity and if they look into our eyes, they can see that we are not sincere. Part of the asceticism of the eye is to bring our eyes into accord with our conscience. Our eyes can learn to lie, to deceive, to hide the true meaning of our words and deeds. In such a case, they are at war with our conscience. In training the eye to do such things, we cause them to help us drown out the voice of our conscience in this life. To bring our eyes into full accord with our conscience is an important thing, because then we can struggle for the purification of the conscience and the eye at the same moment. Our Saviour tells us that the eye is the window of the soul. "If your eye has integrity," He says, "then the whole body is full of light" (Mt.6:22).

It is a useful thing to train the eye to avert itself from those things which tempt us to inappropriate desires and, indeed, we can spare ourselves much inner pain in so doing, but it is a far greater thing, and a more true asceticism of the eye, to train it well for the encounter.

The asceticism of the tongue is also concerned with the encounter, not just avoidance. You can see this easily in the life of your own parish community when the brothers and sisters are brought to sorrow by some person who hurts others with their unbridled and untrained tongue. Apostle James speaks of this with evident sorrow saying that the tongue is a small organ of the body, but it wreaks much sorrow and havoc.[8] We may think that to train our tongue involves keeping it from swearing or cursing, or to avoid saying whatever contemporary mores consider to be "bad words," but this can be simply moralistic. The Pharisees were very diligent about this for moralistic reasons, but they felt free to rebuke people in the most self-righteous and destructive way. Asceticism of the tongue is not merely gaining self-control of what we say and how we say it; our tongues must also be brought into accord with our conscience at the same time that we are struggling for the purification of the conscience. Saint Antony Khrapovitsky reminds us that "perfect holiness is nothing else but perfect compassionate love." True asceticism of the eye and the tongue are part of building a true spirit of love within us, not a moralistic attempt to become "righteous." When we train our tongues so that we do not wound our brothers and sisters, we are not training our tongues to be false, rather we are actually struggling for inner purification — that is, a condition in which the motivation for all that we do or refrain from doing, is sincere love — and gaining control over our tongues to bring them into accord with that inner love, so that when we speak we will speak with love and understanding.

All of these can be completely false and deceptive if we are not also training our "heart" for the same thing. One who rebukes a brother or sister under the delusion that this is being done "righteously" or "for the sake of righteousness" has not yet begun the process inner purification which leads to illumination. Such people have not begun to purify the conscience (the "heart") with repentance and love of the Gospel, but their tongue is indeed in accord with their inner delusion.

One does not even need to count how many times we say something that hurts our brother or sister just from sheer carelessness rather than through any real malice or self righteous egoism. Because we do not have control of our tongues and have not brought them into accord with our struggle for the purification of the heart, we often hurt somebody that we genuinely love, and often through thoughtlessness and carelessness. This all takes place because we have not trained our tongue in an ascetic way and brought it into accord with our heart and our conscience. Everything that I have said about the asceticism of the tongue applies equally to the asceticism of the eye.

Is this not an existential process? Our struggle is to look at our whole person and every way in which we come into communication with other people or any other person. We do not communicate only with our tongue and our eyes, but also with our "heart,"[9] our conscience. So we have to bring the eyes and the tongue into harmony with our conscience while at the same time transforming ourselves inside so that we truly live and behave ourselves in a Christian way. If Sartre and some other existentialists thought that we "create our own essence," the were not completely wrong. We certainly are responsible for the shaping of our particular essence *(hypostasis)*.

When Orthodox Christians approach a fast period, it is not fulfilling to think of it only as placing upon oneself some heavy rule about eating. The lenten period is more meaningful if one can think of it in existential terms and concentrate on what one is doing with the tongue and the eyes. This will reveal much to us about the condition of our hearts, our consciences. If we are undertaking any kind of asceticism with our tongues and our eyes, and seriously thinking about how we may have hurt somebody else, then the lenten period is not only filled with meaning for us, but it becomes a genuinely existential struggle in which we actually take responsibility for our decisions and actions, and truly work at the process of shaping our own particular essence. If, in addition to this, we sincerely contemplate how we might heal ourselves so we no longer do such things, and heal the one whom we have offended or hurt, then we have truly sought and found the meaning in the act of fasting. Let us repeat that true asceticism is not merely about avoidance, it is also about the encounter. Above all, we should think about how every encounter with another human being is always an encounter with Christ Who created them and Who loves and values them.

Orthodox Christian asceticism can sometimes bring sorrow, but it is always a sorrow that blossoms into joy as surely as sincere faith blossoms into everlasting life. The true ascetic acquires a spirit of peace and a spirit of joy in our Lord Jesus Christ. When he has acquired the Holy Spirit, when the Spirit of God indwells him, he does not have a dark countenance but rather a countenance which reflects the joy of the grace he received, or rather that he has become a partaker of. One who has truly acquired the Holy Spirit no longer offends anyone with his eyes or his tongue. The only one who finds offence in him is the one whose conscience he censures, not in words or deeds but in the presence of the Holy Spirit within him. All this is extremely important for holding our community together and holding our parish life together as a life in Christ, and not simply as the life of a society or organization. Moreover, it is vital to us in how we relate, as individuals and as a worshipping community, to the rest of the world: whether we are truly proclaiming to the world the spirit of Christ or, with some legalistic moralism, quite another spirit.

ENDNOTES:

[1]. We might also give a brief and simple definition of *"noetic"*. Theoria is a noetic experience in which we apprehend rather than comprehend. We apprehend meaning by grace rather than comprehend it by the reasoning process

[2]. According to this heresy, which originated with Papism, dogma is developed in all centuries from ideas that were present unclearly, "in seed form" from Apostolic times. This heresy is a justification for papal infallibility and the right of popes to introduce novel dogmas into the Roman Catholic Church. This heresy is espoused in varying forms by some leaders in the Orthodox Church who are advocates of the pan-heresy of Ecumenism. This is one more testimony to the radically heretical nature of Ecumenism.

[3]. We will look later at the reality of the different degrees of suffering that can be encountered even in ordinary asceticism — the inner moral suffering that precedes any real spiritual transformation, but a suffering which is not devoid of joy.

[4]. Indeed, even in some Orthodox literature where icons are described as having some sort of spiritual indwelling, and in some of the hyperbolic discussions of the icon as a "spiritual entity," one approaches, and even passes into, pantheism.

[5]. Often encouraged by Orthodox leaders who are those inclined to sectarianism.

[6]. In fact, when one discusses these problems with some of these self-anointed icon painters, their response is the typically Protestant Fundamentalist response to Scripture, "Each person interprets as he sees fit."

[7]. See *The Icon as Scripture* (Synaxis Press, Dewdney, BC) 2005.

[8]. see Js.3:5-8.

[9]. The word "heart" is used in both the sense of the emotions, as here, and in the sense of the spiritual heart of man, which is the conscience. I do not use the word to refer to the mechanical pump which moves our blood through the body. The physical heart was once thought to be the seat of the emotions because the chemical reactions set off by emotions cause the heart to respond in a way that is profoundly felt physically. Once upon a time, some thinkers thought that the heart was the seat of the soul, as if the soul could be compartmentalized and operate without the rest of the body; Neo-Platonism and Gnosticism still harbour such notions.

III
EXISTENTIALISM AND
FREEDOM OF WILL

For ye have not received the spirit of bondage to fear (Rm.8: 15). There is no fear in love; but perfect love casteth out fear: because fear hath torment. He that feareth is not made perfect in love (1Jn.4:18).

There can be no responsibility without a free will. Existentialism deals with nothing so much as it does with responsibility for our choices in life. This is not a moralistic concept. It is simply a realization that if we are to be free beings, capable of an authentic life, we must be responsible for our own choices rather than being puppets to someone else's dictates. Whether one approaches this in the negative (freedom *from* morality) or in the positive (freedom *of* morality), the exercise of informed free will in our choices is paramount. This is no less true of Orthodox Christian spiritual life than of existentialism in general. It would, however, be an unreasonable hypermoralism to assume that we are completely free or that we can exercise completely free choices about every aspect of our lives. Heredity, accidents of birth such as fetal alcohol syndrome, mental illness, being clinically - transgendered and many other purely incidental and accidental circumstances can curtail our freedom of will and choice. In such cases, only a harsh, rigid fanatic would assign moral responsibility for decisions or actions where freedom of will and choice are severely curtailed or even eliminated. This does not mean that one is not a free being on another level, however. Despite such hindrances in external freedom, one is always free to form an inner orientation toward Christ (according to Whose image we are created), or to orient oneself contrary to Him. Free will in this context is above the level of rational choices and must be identified with man's personal existence and ability to relate to God. This inner freedom belongs to everyone, even those with bankrupt spirits or those who are simply impaired to the degree that they are thereby unable to choose between everyday options in an informed way. Quite apart from the situations we have mentioned, we should not negate the fact that we need the help of grace in so many aspects of our struggle, even in the formation of a positive will and the carrying out of acts of a positive will. Grace, however, never curtails our freedom.

With these caveats in mind, and within the realm of the possible, one may make a free choice only if one knows that there are options and knows what they are. This is the whole point of the story of the forbidden fruit in the Garden of Eden. Knowing that there *are* alternatives, we are obligated to know *what* they are, for only then can we approach an informed and free choice. We may become so informed by means of philosophy, opposing points of view within our own culture and society, from Scripture and illumination by the Holy Spirit, or from all these and other sources. Not every option leads to truth, but an option forced upon one, even if it does lead to truth, does not bring one into conformity or even reconciliation with it. For this, a freely made choice is necessary.[1] No one can be "saved" or made moral by compulsion or law. Conformity and morality are not synonyms.

Orthodoxy calls upon us to exercise our free will in cooperation with God's grace. It does not call upon us to act as puppets or robots to social convention or even to the words of divine revelation. If the mechanical fulfilment of the Ten Commandments or even the whole of the law could have made one "righteous" or bestowed "holiness," there would have been no need for the Incarnation.

No deed which does not proceed from the heart, motivated by love, has any actual moral value.[2] Fulfilling the law out of fear, social pressure or any kind of self-interest could have no genuine moral value. Fulfilling it unselfishly, motivated by love, would require a genuinely free choice that would reflect the image and likeness of God in us. We might choose to obey the written law simply out of fear of punishment, but we need love in order to freely, without coercion, choose to cooperate with divine grace. Cooperating with God's grace does not place us in bondage to mechanical actions nor abolish our free will. We must still make free choices, even those informed by the grace of the Holy Spirit, which inclines us toward certain choices but does not force us to accept them. Choices made under coercion or fear are not accepted in the heart, not made "in spirit," they are not free. They may lead to "correct behaviour" but they cannot make the "heart right with God."[3] Our choices have to be subjective. They have to relate to our own *self* as a cognizant, subjective being, not as an object in any given society. The choice must be our own, not the objective imposition of peer pressure, social convention or interrelationships. Even the choice to enter into or remain in the communal entity of the Church is a free, subjective choice — or it has no ultimate value. The subjective "I" must freely choose to become and remain a part of the objective whole. The loss of one's subjective reality to peer pressure, to please society or even immediate family may result not only in a separation from *self* but may even result in a separation from God. It is certainly a loss of freedom which turns us into an object rather than a sentient, subjective being exercising free will. It precludes constructive cooperation and results in a subjugation and destruction of the "glorious freedom of God's children" (Rm.8:21).

With regard to things about which we have no subjective freedom of choice, we also have no

49

responsibility in them. To be deemed responsible for those things about which we have no subjective choices is to accept Augustine of Hippo's heretical teaching of absolute predestination or even Leibnitz's concept of "fatal necessity." The idea that we would be punished by God for acts and thoughts which we were ignorant of or had no idea were "wrong," is a moral accusation against God, rooted in Gnostic concepts. Indeed, the whole Western Christian notion about the nature of the last judgment and heaven and hell are contrary to both the "nature" of God, the teachings of the holy fathers of the Orthodox Church and even basic human decency. We will discuss existentialism and the last judgment, and the nature of heaven and hell a little later.

The Old Testament covenant was not a legal agreement or treaty between God and Israel. It was a spousal relationship. Israel was the "holy nation" not because of any special holiness in the way its people conducted their daily lives or because of any special righteousness on the part of her rulers. It was "holy" because it was the spouse of the Holy One. Israel was blessed when its people and/or rulers sought to fulfil their spiritual conjugal life with God, and outcast when they did not. A spousal relationship does not require merely the blind obedience to law but the open-eyed cooperative obedience of true love. Without free will we could neither fall into sin nor avail ourselves of redemption; without free will we could not love, and if we could not love, how could we know God Who "is love" (1Jn.4:8)?

THE TREES OF PARADISE

"Meaning" is so often the missing dimension in religious teaching and deliberations. When religious people debate about the creation narrative in Genesis, they leave a certain emptiness. In discussing the Covenant and the Old Testament in general, they so often lapse into moralism without meaning. Their discourses about the creation narrative are almost always concerned with arguing that the story is literally and scientifically accurate. Seldom if ever does one hear an exposition of *meaning* in such discussions. One does not expect to hear much about meaning from atheists who argue about it, but those who profess to be believers have a responsibility to offer it, and they hardly ever do. Nevertheless, this "meaning" speaks of an existential freedom and an existential responsibility on the part of each human person.

We must limit our own discussion here by the purpose and boundaries of this book. The story of the trees of Paradise presents us with a profound existential metaphor — or, if you prefer, a revelation. Let me present this mystery in the form of an excerpt from one of my own Paschal sermons:

"....I would like to call upon you to reflect on the trees of Paradise.

51

"By grace God bestowed life upon mankind but the life He gave to our ancestors was not the life of puppets or robots. He bestowed upon mankind an authentic life. Authenticity of life requires freedom. God created mankind from pure love, but love without freedom is a mere fiction. Love entails trust and respect. This is the awesome mystery of God's love. The all-powerful author of the universe actually respects the freedom of His creatures. He asks in return our love, our trust and our respect.

"Just as there can be no love without freedom, there can be no freedom without choice. When God placed Adam and Eve in Paradise, He placed before them the image of two trees. The first tree is referred to as "the knowledge of good and evil," the second as the "tree of life". The tree of the knowledge of good and evil was withheld from mankind until such time as God knew that Adam and Eve were mature enough to cope with such knowledge. Why was the tree visibly placed before them if they were not to partake of it? Our forebears had the free choice of choosing to respect and trust God, or to mistrust Him and partake of the tree.

"It is obvious that the Tree of Life was also intended for humanity in that this, too, would be given to them in the fulness of time.

"What precisely is the knowledge of good and evil? We know that evil does not have any actual being, that it is not a thing or a substance, that it really does not

52

have any kind of existence. In a certain sense, evil is inauthenticity of life. It is the loss of authentic being. Faith and the struggle for virtue require freedom of will and grant liberty to the faithful struggler. Evil is a form of bondage to fear and hopelessness. It is the vision of non-being or annihilation; it is the fear of death, and this is why Apostle Paul says that fallen humanity is held in bondage to the fear of death (Hb.12:15). This fear is the source of human passions.

"Let us look at what happened to Adam and Eve in Paradise, and we will be able to better understand our own lives and our own bondage. Adam and Eve were created in the image and likeness of God. They were subjective individuals, not mere objects and they had that freedom of will which is necessary for an authentic life, and a natural, unselfish love. Satan deceived them by means of an illusion. He convinced them with a fantasy that they could become something which they were not. Satan convinced them that by betraying God's love and trust, they could become like Him. `If you gain the knowledge of the mystery of good and evil, you will become as God.' `Don't trust God! He has withheld this knowledge from you only from envy, because He does not want you to be like Him.' Adam and Eve lost authenticity of life first of all by exchanging reality for an illusion, by accepting a counterfeit of what they already had. They abandoned what they actually were and accepted a delusion about themselves. One cannot have genuine freedom while living an illusion that deprives one of one's own reality. Satan had `objectified' Adam and Eve. When Adam and Eve lost this authenticity of life, they actually lost a part of their freedom of will. A sea of necessity swept down upon them, forcing them to yield their freedom to the necessities of life and survival. Their choice to heed the temptation of Satan separated them from their intimate communion with God and thus separated them from their union with the source of life. Now, death became a sharp reality to them. Death itself became a source of fear and Satan would increase this fear by tempting humanity to think of death as a complete annihilation. This fear is the source of almost all human passions: it makes us greedy, full of envy, anxious to `have it all now' no matter how destructive that might be. It causes us to ruin the environment and even leads us to our sexual excesses. This fear of death and non-being is the force that breaks the bonds of unselfish love, and makes us egocentric. It robs us of freedom, leads us into delusion, and causes us to live in an illusion instead of in an authentic life.

"In Paradise the Tree of Life was set in the midst of the garden as a symbol of hope and aspiration. It is not the knowledge of good and evil that deifies a human being; it is complete union with the source of life and the indwelling of the Holy Spirit that deifies mankind. Departing from Paradise, humanity lost the vision of the Tree of Life. Man became objectified into an existence filled with delusion and each of us falls constantly into illusions about ourselves. If evil is a loss of authenticity and a separation from the good, a kind of non-being, then all the wickedness and evil into which mankind may fall arises from our own loss of authenticity and our own fear of death as annihilation and non-being. And now we approach holy Pascha and once more we see the Tree of Life set up in our midst, once more we stand in Paradise, that is, in the Paradise of God's love and our faith. And beholding before us the Tree of Life, we are renewed in hope, delivered from the fear of non-being, and once more offered union with the source of life. Now, mankind who was "all his lifetime held in bondage to the fear of death" (Hb.12: 15), is set free once more.

"Yet, without the Resurrection of Jesus Christ, the Cross would not be the Tree of Life, for it is not the *tree* that bestows life, but the *fruit* of the Tree of Life that imparts to us everlasting life.

"Still, the question remains: if God is all-powerful, why was the Incarnation and the suffering of Christ necessary to conquer the power of death? We reply that God did not need to conquer the power of death for His own sake, but for ours. But, if God intended to restore us to authenticity of life, it could not be by depriving us of our freedom. The power of death must be conquered within each one of us, not without our own consent. We still must freely choose between life and death, between freedom and bondage, between hope and fear. The gates of hades must be trampled down in the heart of each one of us as free individuals with responsibility for our own lives. God the Word entering into our humanity in the Incarnation, though being God, also became the first human being to live a fully authentic human life, to resist every temptation of Satan, to live free from the fear of death, to fully love, trust and respect God, and to conquer completely the power of death. He was the first to manifest the "glorious freedom of God's children" (Rm.8:21). He did so visibly before our eyes and, in so doing, bestowed upon us real knowledge. The Cross of Christ, you see, became not only the Tree of Life, but also the tree of the knowledge of good and evil, and this is precisely why the two criminals who were crucified together with Christ were not there by coincidence, but were given as a revelation to us. It was there, on Golgotha, that a choice was made between bondage to death and a return to Paradise. The thief whose heart was open, beholding Christ upon the Cross, somehow in his heart came to the knowledge of the meaning of good and evil. He beheld in Christ the essence of *the good* and understood that separation from *the good* was the essence of evil. At the very moment when it appeared to the world that the death of Christ was evil, the thief freely beheld and chose *the good*. By such an exercise of freedom, he cast off his delusions and returned to authenticity of life: At that very moment, Paradise itself appeared in his heart, even before he heard the promise of Christ: 'Thou shalt be with Me in Paradise.' The Cross of Christ was, for him first of all, the knowledge of good and evil, and his free choice between the two made the Cross the Tree of Life for him.

"God has the power over life and death but even this He does not force upon us against our will, for that would be neither respect nor love. Rather, through His own suffering, His own humiliation, His own meekness, His own ineffable love, He came into our midst and unveiled before us, there on Golgotha, the mystery of the trees of Paradise. As He walked with Adam and Eve in Eden, so He walked amongst us once more and called upon each one of us to make for ourselves the choice which had been offered to our ancestors. It is surely no accident that it was a condemned criminal approaching death on the cross was who was the first to make this choice.

"Brothers and sisters, let us, beholding the Cross on Great and Holy Friday, as we stand before the tomb of Christ, see it first of all as the tree of the knowledge of good and evil. With understanding, let us abandon and lay down before the Cross our delusions about life and our illusions about ourselves, and let us conquer the power of evil by choosing *the good* — and *the good* is our Lord and Saviour Jesus Christ. The moment we firmly make such a choice, the Cross becomes for us the Tree of Life, and on Holy Pascha, as we partake of the *Fruit* of the Tree of Life,

57

Paradise will fill our hearts and we ourselves will be already with Christ in Paradise. We will have, once more, authenticity of life and not mere life."

FREEDOM AND BELIEF

Stone walls do not a prison make,
Nor iron bars a cage.
Minds innocent and quiet take
that for an hermitage.
If I have freedom in my love,
And in my soul am free,
Angels alone that soar above,
Enjoy such liberty.[4]

The great Russian existentialist author Fyodor Dostoevsky was in prison in Siberia when he came to fully believe in God and turn toward the Orthodox Christian faith. He had been deprived of all worldly freedom both political and personal. He had not, however, been denied that free will which is in the very nature of mankind. Someone might assert, with reasonable cause, that our free will is crippled by the fallen condition of our nature, but no one can refute the fact that we do have free will. Dostoevsky came to believe precisely because he saw clear evidence of the essential goodness of humanity under the most dire and dehumanizing of circumstances.

When we speak of freedom to choose, we are not

talking about political freedom or the spiritual freedom of *apathea,* which we address below, nor are we speaking of the "glorious freedom of God's children" that Apostle Paul speaks of to the Romans. All these things are attained to by the faithful who, cooperating with divine grace, struggle toward them. We really are speaking about maintaining an inner freedom which allows us to exercise our free will in making essential choices to be for or against Christ, to honour moral values or reject them. Such decisions to exercise our free will take place within, in the depths of our being. It is possible to compromise such freedom, but we cannot claim not to have free will, no matter how we choose to exercise it.[5]

The purposeful exercise of our inner moral freedom may be curtailed by all kinds of forces, the hypothalamus being chief among them, followed by temptations of Satan. Even our educational system can curtail the proper exercise of this freedom by confusing us about right and wrong, good and evil. The media certainly confuse the activity of our moral freedom by obfuscating the atmosphere in which free will decisions are taken. We advocate being aware of these things and having some idea what to do to free ourselves from certain influences to a level that we can exercise our free will to the greatest degree possible.

In the absence of political freedom, people have maintained an inner freedom, within themselves by becoming insulated in their souls from the forces which coerced their outward actions. These people have had freedom to exercise free will in a way that people who were overcome in spirit by these forces have not had.

Freedom which is not impinged by authorities who force upon one at least external compliance with a value system or religion is desirable, but even with external social or peer pressure, coming into accord with the faith freely is possible. It is a matter of the conscience, the "spiritual heart of man" rather than of an outward compliance hiding an inner indifference or even rejection.

As there can be no responsibility without freedom, so there also can be no authentic faith without freedom. We can believe *in* something in some passive or indifferent way but we cannot have a saving faith without making a free decision to have a committed belief and faith in God—in Jesus Christ. A little later, we will assert that love without commitment is a lie; now we assert that faith without commitment is a delusion.

The catastrophe of "state churches" is sufficient to inform us that religion, faith and belief can be mere cultural affectations. Even without an official state church, religion can become a cultural affectation, as we see in the mythology of the American religious right which teaches that America is somehow a "holy nation," a "new Israel." It can be seen also in nominally Orthodox Christian nations both historically and in our own time.

We may belong to a given Church because it is expected as a matter of patriotic duty without ever being invited to freely come into accord with the essence of that religion. This was the basis of Kierkegaard's assessment of the Danish state church in his own day and one can certainly reach the same assessment of the Orthodox Church of Greece in our own era.

Like authentic morality, faith cannot be coerced or forced. External compliance can be compelled, but there is no benefit without a full accord of the heart with the faith. Having a religion forced upon you or being compelled to fulfil its outward obligations is ultimately more conducive to rebellion and rejection than to a sincere, heartfelt accord—a living, vital faith which leads to inner transformation and salvation. A free exercise of our free will is necessary for a living, saving faith. A person must actually (that is, freely) accept Jesus Christ and accept that the Orthodox Christian faith is the true expression of His gospel, and the true vehicle of the mystery of redemption.

It is really a denial of human free will to attempt to make people observe a given religion by means of coercion, force, fear, compulsion, all of which may obtain an outward conformity, but an inward resentment and rejection. It cannot produce actual faith, it cannot make one actually believe. Faith is a matter of orientation, not a concord with a collection of "facts" or a religious system, nor an exercise of external behaviour.

LOVE AND FREEDOM

Love without commitment is a lie. Love given without freedom is obsession. Love demanded without freedom is psychotic. There can be no authentic love without freedom, and this includes even romantic love which seems to have its own blinding powers of compulsion.

Love may set a boundary to our actions and lead us to constrain ourselves but adherence to the boundary and application of the constraints must be willingly and freely observed, without loss of the freedom to act otherwise. There must be a clear, subjective free will choice among actually existing options.

If the covenant had been a legal agreement or treaty, then only the law could save us. Since, however, the covenant was a spousal relationship, only love can save us. If holiness could be attained by strict observance of a set of laws or moral precepts, then rigidity and cold fanaticism would be the surest path to salvation.[6] But perfect holiness is perfect love, so the only path to salvation is the progressive attainment of unselfish love.[7]

MORALITY AND FREEDOM

Thou shalt love the Lord thy God with all thy heart,
and with all thy soul, and with all thy mind. This is the
first and great commandment. And the second is like
unto it: thou shalt love thy neighbour as thyself. On these
two commandments hang all the law and the prophets.
(Mt. 22:37-40).

Even the "negative" schools of existentialism, such as that of Sartre, certainly do not consider values and morality to be dispensable (adiaphoristic). Both schools, however, oppose value systems which are coerced and allow no freedom to come into accord with them, or reject them, according to the exercise of free will. We must come to grips with the reality that *true morality consists in how well we care for one another, not what sort of behaviour we impose on one another.*

Correct behaviour can be demanded and enforced by law or strong social pressure. We might even go so far as to say that *external moral behaviour* can be enforced or coerced, but morality itself cannot. We will agree with Ortega that the very existence of a state naturally curtails aspects of our freedom because the state of necessity enforces whatever concepts of behaviour are necessary for its survival, or more particularly, whatever concepts are to the best advantage of the most powerful classes in a given state.[8]

Let us specify that we are speaking of the authentic morality which is part of our struggle for salvation, for the state of dispassion and internal purification, not a legalistic code of morality or collective behaviour. Moralism and "herd behaviour" can, in fact, be the result of psychiatric disorders. Legalistic moral codes have more to do with the self-interested preservation of a given social order than with the transformation of the human "heart." And this is the crux of our issue.

From an Orthodox Christian point of view, authentic morality is a matter of the transformation of the inner person. Our Lord Jesus Christ made this abundantly clear in His references to the Pharisees — the most moralistic and externally pious of all the Jews. We wish to make this equally clear to the most moralistic and externally pious Christians.

One does not attain the transformation of the heart and conscience without conscious, willing effort in cooperation with divine grace. No power will force or coerce this inner transformation of a person alienated from the glory of God into a truly moral human being, regenerated by means of such a struggle. This profound inner moral struggle must be undertaken as a free will decision to enter into cooperation (synergism) with the grace of the Holy Spirit, and to struggle even at the cost of an ineffable spiritual suffering, to end one's alienation, one's exile from Paradise. Without subjective freedom, one cannot accomplish this, one cannot even consent to begin it. This struggle is an ontological necessity for us because Adam interjected into our nature an ontological principle of alienation or separation from God and from Paradise.

Yet, how can one desire to return to a homeland that he does not love? How could one endure such an effort to return to the household of a master that he does not love? How could one undertake the journey of such an often painful struggle to return to the embrace of a cruel spouse, unloving and unloved? Fear might send an abused wife back to the clutches of an abusing husband, but it could never sustain such a free moral struggle.

The struggle for true morality can be motivated only by love and undertaken only by a free being who can take a decision based on his own freedom. Without such freedom, there are no alternatives and thus there can be no choices and no decisions.

Let me add that no matter how much one might assert that he is in complete accord with the communal moral code, his accord is, first of all, a result of a subjective choice, and secondly, it is not complete. In the privacy of his own mind, his own self-consciousness, he applies his own concepts of meaning, his own feelings and emotions to his understanding of that code. There will be differences, subtle and large with the understanding applied by others, unless one is a mere object in the communal landscape, a mental automaton incapable of any independent thought or emotions. If that is the case, he can never truly aspire to be an authentic moral human being.[9]

ENDNOTES:

[1]. Actually, this is true even for our children. We can teach them as best we are able, but other sources are teaching them also and they will, like it or not, choose. This is why it is so necessary for us to try to actually live up to the things we teach them.

[2]. Unfortunately, when Christianity became corrupted into a "religion" (amd thus into a series of ideologies), its moral concepts were reduced to a set of laws for appropriate behaviour. In many places, a number of these concepts were merged with Roman concepts of civil good order and legislated into state law as "moral laws." These legislated norms confused the issue of morality. By the same token, "virtue" has come to be understood in a rather saccharine way in the context of moral niceties. Morality thus becomes "relative." It is governed by the requirement of any given society at a defined period in time (e.g., "Victorian morality," etc.).

Virtue is the quest for the Good (as we will discuss a little later) while true Christian morality (which is related to salvation) is to willingly come into accord with the Good *by means of a transformation of the heart*. Ethics equals correct behaviour set by some rules, usually contemporary standards. Morality is a transformation of the heart to accord with the spirit of the Good — or if you will, the spirit of the immediate, personal teachings of Christ.

[3]. Nor can the Latin notion of "absolution" from "wrong" choices. There is no need for absolution, which is essentially a magical idea. There is a need for repentance, which is an expression of a heartfelt desire to take the "right" decisions, to "rethink"one's perspective and "reorient" oneself toward the good, toward Jesus Christ. Repentance is not an apology or absolution for breaking a law, it is simply a desire to turn one's life around followed by action to try to do that with the help of grace.

[4]. *To Althea From Prison*, Richard Lovelace (1618-1658).

[5]. Of course, no amount of free will can help us to become free of the power of death and the temptations of the Evil-One, since only Jesus Christ could do that. A free will choice within us can, however, unite us with Christ so that we may share in those victories He has wrought for us.

[6]. See *Point of Faith Nr. 9: The Nature and Meaning of Sin* (Synaxis Press, 1978)

[7]. For an indispensable discussion of this subject, see St Antony (Khrapovitsky's) "The Moral Idea of the Dogma of Redemption" in *The Moral Idea of the Main Dogmas of the Church* (Synaxis Press, 1976).

[8]. Jose Ortega y Gassett, *Concord and Liberty*. (The Norton Library, N.Y., 1963. Tr. Helene Weyl) pp.33-38.

[9]. I am reminded of the idea expressed by Jose Ortega y Gasset that "...minor divergencies serve but to confirm and consolidate the underlying unanimity of the collective existence" (*Concord and Liberty*. The Norton Library, N.Y., 1963. Tr. Helene Weyl) p.16.

67

IV
FREEDOM AND
CHOOSING VALUES[1]

The world as we see it when we peer through the windows of our "cave" is reality. It is our primary reality. Stereoscopic, colour windows bring, not Plato's shadows, but tangible, physical reality into the cave of our skull to be interpreted and inscribed on the walls of our grey matter like paintings on the walls at Altamira. The things which are thus apprehended by our senses and comprehended by our minds become the first level of awareness outside the immediate awareness of our own self-existence. This experience of sensual perception enters into the realm of our own self-awareness and, because by the nature of our being, we necessarily see and interpret in relation to our own *self*. Subjectivity is the nature of our being because of that very self-awareness that makes us humans. Objectivity must be the result of a conscious effort but even what we view objectively is interpreted with our subjective concepts of meaning.

We do not establish our values on the basis of this primary reality, but on the realities we learn to perceive beyond it. We are not speaking of an abstract, metaphysical realm of ideal forms but of an understanding of interrelationships that we learn to perceive beyond surface appearances. We may intuitively value the beauty of nature because it pleases our senses but we learn to value nature in and of itself only when we learn of the interrelatedness and inter-dependency of all existing things, including ourselves, within its framework.

We learn to value our own humanity, humanity itself and its civilisations, cultures and institutions from various sources. If we pay attention, we are presented with a choice of value systems drawn from these and competing cultures and civilisations. These may include the Bible, the Koran, the Upanishads and various interpretations of them, or a rejection of all of them. We may choose our values based on our own analysis or by the convincing arguments of others, but choose we must. Our choosing will remain the subjective action of a free human individual, but it will be based on our secondary encounter with reality which concerns us with the meaning of the primary and of our place in relation to it. We are negotiating in our minds the meaning of our existence and our ultimate destiny. We are involved in an existential activity. We are free, moral beings only insofar as we exercise a free moral choice. Here, I mean that we must make a choice not pre-conditioned by any totalitarianism or absolutism in which we may have been raised or have been long exposed to. We may choose one set of dogmatic precepts over another, but the important matter is that we come into accord with them freely and not by compulsion. Ultimately, our choices are made, altered, enhanced or changed by the subjective perception of our relationship with God, the universe, the world, nature, humanity, our nation, our community, our family and with our own *self*. Even when a group of people fully accepts the same dogmatic system and religious principles, the values individuals in the group express often differ in both subtle and dramatic ways. It is our subjective perception of the relationship of our *self* to other entities that forms the divergence. We might paraphrase existentialist philosopher Maurice Merleau-Ponty and assert that the choices led to by this subjective perception derive from our "presence at the moment when things, truths, values are constituted for us. That perception is a nascent logos that teaches us outside all dogmatism...that summons us to tasks of knowledge and action...."[2] Interestingly, this is reminiscent of Saint Andrew of Crete who, in his *Gre at Can o n*, says: "The ladder [of Jacob]...is a model of undertaking by action and ascending by knowledge. Be renewed by living in activity, knowledge and contemplation."[3] Again, in the same ode of the Canon, Andrew of Crete tells us to use the story of Leah and Rachel as a type of knowledge and action. Knowledge, he says, is obtained with much active labour. Here, the saint is not offering dogmatic propositions but calling us to an existential responsibility. He is calling us to tasks of knowledge and action through being present to the truths he is offering us.

From our Orthodox Christian perspective, the task of knowledge and action that we are called to is to apply our *energy* to the formation of our particular essence, to struggle to ascend toward a noetic perception[4] which transcends sensual perception, to assimilate a reality which transcends all sensual and rational experience and even every dimension of "reality." We are called upon to strive toward a reality which is apprehended noetically, outside the realm of every dimension of perceptible phenomena and which informs the soul beyond the mind of infinite value which can be measured by no human or earthly criteria. This should by no means be thought of as advocating a radical dualism in the nature of man, nor a condescension to Plato's *noetos kosmos*. The process of learning and memory can be observed through a microscope and seen and measured with modern medical scanning devices. There is no negation of the actual reality of the world we see, but there is a dimensionality, spoken of by St Maximos the Confessor. There is the seen and the unseen, the perceptible and the imperceptible, the finite and infinite, the created and the uncreated. If Niketas Stethatos is correct that when the soul departs the body, it takes the memories and perceptions with it, then this is not because of any dualism, but a miracle of God's grace. Indeed, the very departure of the soul from the body, this "sundering of the person" which

71

we refer to as death, occurs only because of God's will and ultimately for our benefit. No one can claim to know of a certainty that the mind and the brain have any separateness, but it is certain that the mind works through and by means of the brain. We are quite certain that the hippocampi are the key structures in memory formation and that long term memory is stored in the neo-cortex. Memory is a function of activity-dependent changes in neuronal connections. It is not the function of a dualistic "mind" which functions separately from the brain or the soul. There is no sort of Gnostic dualism in the organism of man; we are speaking of dimensionality, not dualistic existences.

We may choose the values given us within the framework of the doctrines and dogmas of the faith, but we know from experience that even among the most devout Orthodox Christians, the values thus engendered are perceived in a subjective manner and are not all the same for each Orthodox person. For some, universal health care is a moral value of the very highest order — a "universal obligation" dictated not only by the moral imperative of Christ that we cite at the beginning of this section, but by the First Ecumenical Council — while for others it is seen in a negative light. We have a whole scope of such variations. The important thing for us is that we come into a freely chosen accord with the basic values of repentance, regeneration and ascent from purification

72

to illumination to glorification — to strive toward a noetic perception in which even the very concept of "value" vanishes in the face of the love and glory of God. This is the value we have chosen, this call to ascend from glory to glory (2Cor.3:18). All the primary and secondary levels of value are transitory, finite platforms. Of greatest importance to us is that we have made the choice, in an informed and free manner, not by compulsion, but by a response of love to love and a desire for the God in Whose image and likeness we were created. The choice is existential, and we pursue it in an existential manner, by means of moral struggle *(askesis; podvig)* in cooperation with divine grace.

We will discuss the four dimensions of moral value, or rather, value and morals in the last chapter of this book.

APATHEA AND FREEDOM

As we have mentioned, existentialism requires us to make value and moral choices freely, without coercion, without being puppets. We may become convinced to take a decision other than the choice we have been following by many forms of evidence or arguments, but the choice should be made by an exercise of our will, freely made.

From an Orthodox Christian point of view, one of the greatest of oppressors and autocrats is our own passions. Often, when a person thinks that his or her choices are being freely made, deeper reflection and more reasoned contemplation will reveal that one is actually acting under the compulsion of the passions. We do, in fact, become puppets to our passions, being both coerced and bullied by them.[5] So long as the passions have this power in our lives, we do not have complete freedom and many of our choices are not being made on the basis of reason and free will. Only the liberation of our will from the totalitarianism of our passions can make us truly free. Liberation from this bondage is part of the great Orthodox Christian existential struggle.

The path of *apathea* — dispassion — is the path to a freedom of the spirit that precedes the ultimate freedom promised us by God. As Adam interjected into the symmetry of the universe the ontological principle of alienation (sin), and sin interjected death (separation from God), so Jesus Christ has interjected the principle of resurrection and life into our nature, into the symmetry of the universe (Rm.5:12-15). We are in bondage to the first primarily through the passions, and liberated into the second by the struggle, in cooperation with grace, for the state of dispassion and purification.

This struggle is described for us in many Orthodox Christian texts so we need not discuss it in detail, only to point out that it is the focus of Orthodox Christian existentialism.[6] The more complete the dispassion, the greater the freedom. Freedom from the passions is essential for moral perfection and, as Paul tells us, "This is God's will for you, even your perfectionment." Fortunately, we do not have to fully attain to such perfection in order to find salvation. If we make a genuine, sincere effort, Christ has made up the difference for us.

Ultimately, emotions, which cause us so much suffering at times, come to be controlled and overruled by an illumined reason; a reason illumined by the grace of the Holy Spirit and informed by a purified conscience. On the other hand, like Jaime in Carlos Fuentes' novel, *The Good Conscience*, we can crush or close out the influence of the good direction of our conscience and come into accord with a frame of mind quite contrary to it. As with Jaime, we can then convince ourselves that having come into accord with the conventions of our social status is the essence of a good conscience.

THE DIMENSIONS OF VALUE AND THE THRESHOLDS OF VIRTUE

The modern use of the word "value" is actually relativistic and suited to a pluralistic, secular society. However, it is now used by most Protestants and "family values" advocates as well as philosophers of ethics and it has become understood as encompassing the moral standards of a given group or society. We would prefer to use the word "virtue" throughout this section of this book, but the term is too easy to misunderstand because of its contemporary context. In its classical sense, virtue (*arete* in Greek) indicates the acquisition of the good and the quest for excellence (in a certain context). In the 1700s a mercantile paradigm entered the vocabulary and the idea of value, rather than virtue arose. Since that time, there has been a "science of value" referred to as *axiology,* a term which indicates "worth." The concept of value and values is so complex and varies so much from one school of philosophy to another that we are not going to deal with a concrete definition of it. We will use the term "value" and "values" in discussing the first two dimensions, explaining their meaning in our context as we go. In general, the term will indicate a culturally determined moral value where that understanding is obvious.

We will ease into the use of the concept of virtue a little later at the point where "value" and "values" simply will not do. Since the 18th century, "value" has come to be used on a regular basis and the term "virtue" is so easily misunderstood as exceptionally proper behaviour in a moralistic sense. Unless we shift from the concept of *value,* to the idea of *virtue,* however, we cannot reasonably approach the "fourth dimension" discussed in philosophy. Basic behavioural traits may be discussed in terms of value, and they will be found to be fairly universal in humanity, but will not be concerned with the idea of "the good" or the

76

pursuit of excellence.

The question of value and the concepts of morality occupies a prime place in the history of philosophy. In general, this has been a speculative attempt to make sense and pattern of human behaviour. Lawmakers from Hammurabi, Moses and Solon to the Communist idea of the "homus sovieticus" have attempted to control and channel human behaviour. In the modern consumerist age, corporations have sought to understand human behaviour in order to manipulate and exploit it.

The experiences of all these groups and of modern social sciences inform us of at least a universal commonality of human nature. From an Orthodox Christian perspective, we would say that there is, in fact, one universal nature of all mankind. Anthropologists support this doctrine, though they usually reach different conclusions from it than we do.

Lawmakers have sought to force and enforce varying degrees of behavioural conformity to the immediate needs of a given society in specific circumstances at different periods of history under the guise of morality. Philosophers (with some exceptions) have sought to elevate the human perspective so that norms of behaviour are based on higher reason and wisdom. This was the basis of Socrates' fatal attempt to displace the Homeric heroes, warriors famous for their skills at deceit, lying and killing people, with a higher ideal: heroes of wisdom and self-control. Plato placed Socrates at the head of this new "hall of fame." Almost all religions have sought a divine basis for establishing control of human behaviour by appeal to transcendental commands. Combining religion with law and rationalism, we come to two extreme views of responding to the problem of inner human suffering — the passions — of man, and behaviour antithetical to the best interests of a given society. At one extreme, the moralistic approach is to punish human suffering, to punish those whose passions become manifested in open behaviour as well as those who actually become criminals. The other extreme is the overreaction against moralistic excesses, particularly in the most democratic societies, by relativising and minimalising human values and moral concepts.

On the other hand, Buddhism and other ascetic philosophies have sought to negate the passions, this inner suffering which so easily becomes manifested in destructive ways, by cutting oneself off from all connections and relationships which appear to support or enhance such sufferings or passions. Negating the feelings and emotions with meditation and mental asceticism, backed by physical asceticism, is a method of dealing with the human passions practised from Japan and China to Europe, by every religion and transcendental philosophy we know of.

Orthodoxy would see the solution in recognizing these sufferings for what they are and struggling to rise above and beyond them in a process of inner healing.

The primary means for doing this is struggling to replace self-love or selfish love with unselfish love and, ultimately, a cosuffering love which helps to heal others of such suffering or passions. Indeed, for Orthodox Christians, this concept of cosuffering love is seen as the mystery of redemption. Ultimately, any true morality depends on how well we care for one another, rather than on what kind of behaviour we force upon ourselves and others. The conquest of the passions does not lie in the blotting out of the mind or in a cold, meaningless detachment, but in the healing of the whole person.

Since our approach in this book has been to examine questions from a point of view which relates to a specific system of thought — existentialism — we will try to anticipate and respond in advance to questions about the main approaches to understanding value and moral concepts. Following Robert Hilary Kane, we will examine briefly and in a simplified form four dimensions of value or values assessment (though we do not follow his formulae exactly).

First, however, it may be useful to examine the difference between *subjective choices* and *subjectivism* in order to avoid confusion. We mentioned the subjective relativism of Sartre and Bertrand Russell earlier. We classed Sartre in the "negative" school of existentialism, yet we have asserted that our choices of value systems and concepts of the moral must be free, subjective choices. The subjective choice of values by a free individual indicates "coming into accord with." Moreover, subjectivity in this context indicates a free choice in terms of having weighed alternatives and come to accept that alternative which one feels is true. This is, in a sense, a conversion experience. Coming freely into an accord with a value system is the acceptance of the principles of that system, notwithstanding that in every system, there are differing perspectives, even various schools.

Subjectivism such as that of Sartre and Russell, holds that there are no objective grounds for ethical judgments of right or wrong and that what seems right to a given individual is right for him or her without appeal to any other authority and in the face of universal concepts. It is a matter of creating a personalized ethical system which may or may not apply to anyone else in your society. Russell goes somewhat further in asserting that all knowledge is limited to science and science says nothing about "values." His subjectivism carried him to assert that to deem something "good" is merely to affirm one's own personal desires.

To the modern reader who is not involved in the technical vocabulary of philosophy, terms like "subjective" and "objective" often have meanings that are different than, or even the reverse of, those given them by specialists. In the understanding of many people, it is being *objective* that leads to moral relativism, while being subjective assigns to your own values an absolutist universality.

With these provisions and caveats in mind, let us look, in a very simplified form, at the dimensions of value. To Robert Kane's[7] four, I have added two: a "pre-first dimension" and a fifth dimension, "transcendental value."

1. Pre-First Dimension

The four dimensions of value pertain to those values or moral concepts unique to sentient humans. However, there are some natural values shared by other creatures, particularly by other mammals, and these are values pertaining to survival. They also appear to be the footing upon which the foundation of higher dimensions of value are built up. Many animals behave in ways that we would consider morally good. Some species groom one another, which is a mutual benefit. Some share food, many display parental love and care, and not a few have monogamous relationships for life. Male and female in a number of species share the rearing of their children. Gibbon monkey males are outstanding parents, tending, nur turing and carrying their young about.

Tribal behaviour, which is the origin of complex social entities, goes beyond cooperative hunting. Chimpanzees and some other species demonstrate tribal relationships that in sentient humans would be considered either moral or immoral. Tribal entities

81

share food and defence, experience a kind of rudimentary patriotism, can exhibit kindness, and 1also commit murder and genocide, and the males commit aggressive rape.

We like to class all behaviour in non-human species "instinctive" and automatic, but in man, we class the same behaviour as "moral" and "immoral." While which behaviour is classed in which way varies with time and culture among humans, many are universal among all humans. Nevertheless, there are some stark differences. Suicide has been the only moral and honourable thing to do in some societies under some circumstances, and regarded with horror and one of the ultimate immoral actions in others. Infanticide has been acceptable in some cultures, loathed in others. Slavery has occurred in every society. The sexual exploitation and abuse of women has been acceptable in many if not most societies at one time or another. Nevertheless, in most Western societies, all these things are looked upon as degrading and considered to be "devalue" at the very least.

Behaviour that is bare survival based, we have classed as pre-first dimensional. The four dimensions of value belong only to sentient humanity, not because we are prepared to assert that no other animals are cognizant, but because we believe that man has an actual moral conscience and that only humans can make informed choices with cognizance of long-term effects on long range plans. Man can aspire to higher, better and purer. From our point of view, this is so because the "image and likeness" of God are implanted in the nature of man. Mankind is essentially good and not depraved, fallen but not without the trace of the divine image, alienated from God, but not cut off from Him.

2. First Dimension: Experience

At the primary level, infants begin to establish a concept of values on the basis of simple experiences. Pain is bad, lack of pain is good. Being hungry is bad, being fed is good. Behaviour that elicits positive reactions from parents is good, behaviour that draws a negative reaction is bad (although they may reverse this judgment in teenage years).

Baruch Spinoza expressed experience-based values as "value" and "devalue" experiences. He included among "value experiences" such things as delight, enjoyment, love and ecstasy. As "devalue experiences," he includes such things as hate, grief, disappointment, humiliation, etc. All these may be highly personalized values based on our emotional reactions to given experiences. However, mankind has the ability to learn from the cumulative experience of any social entity he belongs to, and in more modern times, to assimilate values from the experience of a variety of far different cultures.

At the primary level, experience gives us a sense

and emotion-based concept of "value" and "devalue," often at the utilitarian level.

There are, in our view, certain innate moral principles in the conscience of man that have developed along with, and partly because of the human ability to be cognizant of, analyze and build on not only his own experience, but the experience expressed in traditions handed down from previous generations. Mankind has a moral foundation of viable, sentient, interpretable *tradition*. This is why we are able to pass into the second dimension of value.

3. Second Dimension: Considered Behaviour

Traditional values and moral concepts are not always appropriate. We mentioned before that some traditions would tell us that suicide is the only moral and honourable thing to do under certain circumstances. A high value is placed on this honourable behaviour and kamikaze pilots earned instant entry into heaven because of it. Sometimes traditional values contain the poison of our worst prejudices and injustices. It is here, in the second dimension that we begin to give consideration to the meaning of experience-based values and weigh the appropriateness of those traditional values which are received from the experience of earlier generations. In this dimension, we begin to examine the purpose of values and apply them to considered behaviour. We can now examine and test values and moral concepts.

First dimension value experiences help us form a pattern of assessment, but we need patterns which are beyond "how it makes us feel," and beyond those values necessary for basic survival. We need patterns that help us assess value in terms of end results and that go beyond good and bad, into more abstract applications. If we are to rise to this next dimension in our discussion, and pass into more abstract applications, we really must begin to think in more Orthodox terms and consider the use of the word "virtue." Considered behaviour, making clear moral and value choices for our lives, brings us toward the concept of virtue. If we wish to shift now to the idea of "virtue," let us suggest that, at this point, we would call upon people to place the quest for *virtue* as their highest value. We have decided to make this shift at the fourth level for reasons that might become evident as we go.

4. Third Dimension: Self-Defining Behaviour

Value acquisition certainly includes things our parents teach us as we grow up, although some might not consider this "experience value." We learn value concepts from others, from school, from our reading, our worship and a host of other sources. Ultimately, however, we enter second dimension values when we begin to purposely shape our behaviour, our actions and our plans — particularly long term plans — with these values in mind. We now have "considered behaviour," considered in terms of a value system or set of values. Extending this over time and letting our values become more deeply a part of our lives leads us to the next, or third, dimension of value. This is the level at which our values actually help to define who and what we are. We are now thinking in terms of ethical and unethical as well as good and bad, as they help shape our character and define our personality and our role and position in society. At this level, we may call our values "ideals." Above all, from an Orthodox Christian point of view, our concept of value must now yield to the traditional understanding of "virtue." If virtue conotates seeking the Good, then our considered behaviour and our self-defining value as Orthodox people must become focused upon this ascending virtue. We may choose as we will, but this is the orientation asked of all who desire to come into accord with the Orthodox Christian "value system." Nevertheless, we must accept that, at this level, not all in modern society will even comprehend this concept, let alone agree with it. Purposeful behaviour in modern times is more likely to be aimed at materialistic targets rather than excellence in the sense of virtue. We must also leave the discussion of seeking the Good for our fifth dimension.

Our values help define us as human beings. The way we *apply* them also has much to say about who and what we are. We can understand this from a purely secular example. In one of his lectures, philosopher Robert Hilary Kane gave the example of a tribal hunter. He hunts for food as a matter of necessity. However, he also considers seeing his family hungry to be "bad," while feeding them is "good." The matter becomes more complex than this. The hunter also takes pride in his skill with a bow because this says something about him. He may be able now to define himself as a good hunter, a good provider for his family and a man who is valuable to the tribe. This is not simply a matter of status, rather it is part of the way he assesses himself and also of the way his neighbours define him.

This is the dimension in which we value the virtues of aesthetics, art, music, medicine, etc. We diversify our context of good, bad, negative, positive, morally right or wrong, patriotism, loyalty, etc. We may also re-evaluate religious or spiritual values and seek to come to more purposeful and considered choices, because this sphere reflects so deeply on our self-definition.

While value in this dimension may be fairly objective, in the larger scheme of humanity it remains relative to our own culture, sub-group, community or whatever organizations we may belong to, and certainly to our religious and political affiliations.

We should add that, when we are making choices among alternatives, we are making subjective choices, but they will then become more or less objective in terms of the group or culture they help fit us into. Making a choice of a value system may be *subjective,* the values themselves may be *objective*. We subjectively choose to come into accord with a value system, whereupon, we objectively become part of the community defined by those values. Our self-identification includes identifying ourselves with that community. For Orthodox Christians this means shifting from the secular or even a religious view of "value" and "values" to the ideals of virtue and "seeking the Good" consistent with Orthodox tradition.

Can we go beyond this into fourth dimension value, a level which concerns objective worth and universally applicable values, even universal human obligations? Hume and the sentimentists[8] certainly felt that we can. We will let Hume take us into the fourth dimension, though we may define it somewhat differently than Spinoza, Kane and others.

And here, we will part company with most of the philosophers who discussed these dimensions before us, but acknowledge that not everyone who approaches this level of value will keep company with us.

As we enter this fourth dimension, virtue will signify "the pursuit of excellence."

5. Fourth Dimension: Universal Worth

The fourth dimension of value is supposed to deal with value that is universally applicable and valid. In theory, the fourth dimension would make Kant's Categorical Imperative workable. The difficulty of Kant's notion of each of us becoming a legislator or at least proctor of universal moral value is that, first of all, there are so many variables in the way people understand value. Secondly, many values (or, moral values) are good from one point of view, not good from another. Some actions may be *devalue* (or, immoral) under some circumstances but not under others. Being in love is good, but not if it is with someone else's wife. Suicide is an absolute sin in some societies but in others it has been a noble act with high value, at least under some circumstances. Many philosophers doubt, therefore, that we can ascend to a fourth dimension of value, others, such as true relativists, question the very existence of this level. From a secular or purely philosophical point of view, this matter really is debatable.

At this point, let us assert that only virtue, properly understood, and not "value" can have any universal application and validity. Thus "virtue" and not "value" can take us into the fourth dimension. Let us begin with a primary level of virtue, the pursuit of excellence. The pursuit of excellence is not connected with ideas of competition and "getting ahead" in any material sense. We are speaking about aspirations, not ambitions. Indeed, ambition is the catafalque of aspirations. The pursuit of excellence has to do with the higher inclinations of man. A sculptor might begin a carving with only the idea of how much profit he can make from it as a primary motive. This is certainly not the pursuit of excellence, but a betrayal of that pursuit. To create a work of beauty that brings him higher and to greater perfection in his talents and heartfelt calling is the pursuit of excellence of the sculptor: to create the most beautiful work possible, not to "be the best that he can be," this is the pursuit of excellence. The pursuit of excellence in our inter-human relations, in the development of our character, our personality, our particular essence *(hypostasis)*, our moral conscience, this is the true meaning of virtue, although virtue will bring us to a higher dimension yet.

I would like to suggest that, in this context, Christ's moral imperative, "do unto others as you would have them do unto you" (the golden rule), and His own Categorical Imperative ("love the Lord thy God....and love thy neighbour as thyself") are more workable than Kant's imperatives because we are provided with a means for actually accomplishing them. Moreover, the different categories and qualities of love are fairly well defined in common over most societies, and murderers, torturers, extortionists, etc, do not want others to do the same to them. Above all, Christ's Categorical Imperative, unlike Kant's, does not assume that each one of us can become a legislator of universally applicable maxims of behaviour.

We will assert that from an Orthodox Christian perspective, the fourth dimension does not deal with "value," except insofar as it calls upon us to regard virtue (in the classical sense of the word) as of the greatest value. Nevertheless, let us continue in the terminology of philosophy for the moment.

Hume and other empiricists of the "sentiment" school believed that there are universally felt sentiments that are positive value from any point of - view. I will agree with Hume that this level exists and also with his conclusion that humans are essentially good, while recognizing (as Hume does also) man's inner struggle with good and evil. I think that Hume was also correct in suggesting that certain values are innate in the human nature and that, barring some of the things that derail them, are universal and manifested on a pan-human level. Hume, as an atheist, would have a somewhat different understanding of the source and nature of these values than we do. In fact, we would refer to these values as "virtues." Since they are "virtues," we will assert that virtue itself impels us to strive for excellence in them; indeed to struggle to perfect them in ourselves.

Let me be clear at this point that we are not talking about a universal, absolutist moral code. We are talking about innate virtues that define us as truly human: kindness, mercy, love, an inclination toward God, etc,[9] all of which have a direct opposition in our fallen nature which we consider to be vices or define as "sin" because they actually separate us from God. We expect to find these virtues in everyone who is not either psychopathic or given over wholly to the power of Satan.

Speaking as an Orthodox Christian, I will assert that these universal sentiments which we call virtue, are impressed in our being from the time of creation, not forced upon us by a legal code. We say that humanity was created "in the image and likeness of God" and Saint John Damascene explains the qualities this implies, "The phrase `After His image,' has reference to free will and intellect...whereas `after His likeness indicates a likeness in virtue'."[10] No matter how dimmed it may have become in us, every human being is "in the image and likeness of God" because there is only one, single nature of all mankind and it is imprinted with certain virtues and an inclination toward virtue.

Moralists might distort the concept of fourth dimension value into absolutes, defined by their own particular values or interpretations of value, to which people must be forced to conform. Prohibition is a good example, apartheid might be another. Societies need laws governing behaviour to the degree necessary for the preservation of that society. So far as personal morality is concerned, it cannot be enforced by external law any more than Prohibition could succeed. I will agree with Hume that the innate good "sentiments" in humanity can be enhanced and strengthened through moral education,[11] but choices regarding them must be implemented by each subjective individual. We cannot agree with sentimentist Adam Smith (the Karl Marx of capitalism) that man's good sentiments will limit his exploitation of others, since experience has taught us otherwise. Karl Marx was more correct in asserting that economics changes the way people think and that the market place would erode human benevolence and morality.

Sympathy, compassion, distress at the pain and suffering of others — even if it is limited to the people of your own "tribe" — are sentiments that we are all familiar with. They appear to be among the innate sentiments in mankind and someone without these positive dispositions is considered to be perverse or mentally deranged.[12] Consequently, we will agree with Hume and other empirical sentimentists, and with ethicist Robert Hilary Kane that there is a fourth dimension of value in which we find positive emotions of universal value and negative emotions of universal devalue.

Hume was an atheist who would see "natural causes" as the basis of this universal value, Adam Smith and the Deists might see them as immutable laws established by a remote deity who created us and then stopped paying attention to us. We have already asserted that our universal, positive sentiments are innate because we are created in the image and likeness of God. Our universal devalue "opposites," we would assert, are results of the fall from unity with God. I suggest that the desire to know God is also

93

innate in mankind and that there is circuitry in the brain for spiritual knowledge the same as there is for other survival needs.

We pass through and, to one degree or another, become aware of these dimensions as we grow from infancy to adulthood and as we develop our thinking. We sometimes change our perspectives on them and change our ideas about the value or devalue of specific emotions, sentiments and/or actions.

We have resolved to agree with those who assert that there is a fourth dimension but I will argue that it is beyond the pale of mere value. It has to do with virtue, and we can ascend into it and make use of it. I wish to advance the idea now of a fifth dimension of value, a dimension of transcendent value. For us, this dimension will relate to those who are conscious of God. Deists and atheists may desire a "spirituality," but this is not the subject of our fifth dimension. For us, the highest value is redemption, reunion with God in Jesus Christ and the indwelling of the Holy Spirit.

6. Fifth Dimension: Transcendent Value; Virtue and the Quest for the Good

Our fifth dimension pertains to eternal value which transcends all earthly value. We are going to speak of it in Orthodox Christian terms which preclude any of the moral fascism of scholastics and fundamentalists. Our struggle is not for some brand of "morality" or

94

for some acceptable value system. The quest for the Good is the struggle for true reunion with God in Jesus Christ. Every positive thought and action we take in this journey is in the category of virtue, not of value. When we speak of "seeking the Good," one may be reminded of the words of Canadian philosopher George Grant: "Good" is "good which we do not measure and define, but by which we are measured and defined."[13] This is a profoundly Orthodox point of view. Seeking the Good is a self-defining virtue for Orthodox Christians.

In the preceding pages we have discussed many aspects of the Orthodox concept of transcendent "value" already. We do not want to restate what has already been said, but we must refer to it briefly in order to set it all both in the context of the dimensions of value, which may open the idea to the secular mind, and in the context of virtue and the love of the Good, which more clearly expresses the Orthodox mind.

Whatever concepts of value and morality we have chosen to guide us in our lives, we are called upon to transcend them. Morality as the fallen nature understands it can be reduced to a code of law and compliance can be at least outwardly enforced in many ways. Jesus Christ informed us, however, that outward conformity was not the purpose of the matter: if you have mentally consented to a deed, then you have committed it in your heart (Mt.5:28). Coming into accord with the principle of virtue begins in the "heart" and then becomes manifested in our whole lives both visibly and internally, just as we are sanctified, beginning with the "heart" and gradually encompassing our whole being.

Transcendent "value" can only be understood in the context of "virtue." It focuses us on the three major stages in the life process of the sincere believer: purification of the conscience, illumination of the inner person and glorification of the whole person. The ultimate "value" is *theosis*, being filled with the uncreated *Energy* of God, having the fulness of the indwelling Holy Spirit. As one ascends along this path, one rises above all earthly moral concepts into the certain knowledge that perfect holiness consists in nothing else but perfect love; perfect righteousness consists in the fulness of co-suffering love in Christ. None of the four dimensions of value that we have discussed should be considered "absolute." We may view them only as platforms for ascent. All the values we espouse, all the moral conduct we seek to observe, all these things are for us only tools or instruments in the struggle to acquire the indwelling of the Holy Spirit. If we truly acquire the Holy Spirit then we fulfil by nature those things which before were given to control our nature. We fulfil the demands of a pure conscience without ever judging or condemning anyone else, simply because godly love opposes the negative impulses within our fallen nature and co-suffering love in Christ causes us to see the falls and passions of others as genuine suffering in need of healing. Our hearts can then embrace their suffering so that we might serve for their healing if by any means an opportunity is given. Our whole perspective of value, values and morality is so changed that we can hold no arrogance, no self-righteousness, no condemnation, but only an all encompassing co-suffering love for humanity, indeed for the whole universe.

FREEDOM OF WILL AND
THE LAST JUDGMENT:
HEAVEN AND HELL

This subject might logically be discussed following our section on *Orthodox Theology and Existentialism.* Since, however, it has a great deal to do with the subjective freedom we have been talking about, and particularly subjective moral free will, we may discuss it at this point. For our purposes, these discussions would not be complete if we did not discuss the ultimate destiny of man from an Orthodox Christian perspective. We will have discussed *theosis* as the end of our moral struggle, but since images of heaven and hell and the final judgment permeate so much of religious and philosophical thought, we must say something about these subjects also. Here again, we will find an existentialist theme in the Orthodox Christian understanding of the nature of these things. In particular, we will find that the matter of freedom and responsibility for choices dominates the true Christian concept of judgment and of hell and that the oppressive, tyrannical juridicalism of Western thought is not significant. Western Christian thought about these matters is dominated by pagan myths, especially those of Hellenism. It may be that the Western understanding of hell was shaped, to a degree, by the myth of Er which Plato offers as a condescension at the end of the tenth book of his *The Republic*.

Hell is not a place created by God for the punishment of sinful people. Indeed, hell is not a place at all, but a state of being. For those who may experience hell after the last judgment, that state or condition will be a product of their own conscience, a result of a free choice which they themselves have made. Hell is an affirmation, not a rejection. No one experiences hell because he has been rejected by God or deprived by God of His love. Hell is an affirmation of our own choices, of the fact that God respects us and respects our choices for all eternity. If it is in any way a rejection, then it is a result of our own rejection of God's unchangeable love as St Isaak of Nineveh instructs us:

> *I also maintain that those who are punished in Gehenna are scourged by the scourge of love. Nay, what is so bitter and vehement as the torment of love? I mean those who have become conscious that they have sinned against love suffer greater torment thereby than by any*

fearsome punishment which can be conceived. For the sorrow caused in the heart by sin against love is more piercing than any torment. It would be improper for a man to think that sinners in Gehenna are deprived of the love of God. Love is the offspring of knowledge of the truth which, as is commonly confessed, is given to all. The power of love works in two ways: it torments sinners, even as happens here when a friend suffers from a friend; but it becomes a source of joy for those who have observed its duties. According to my understanding this is the torment of Gehenna: bitter regret. But love inebriates the souls of the sons of heaven by its delectability.[14]

Let us emphasize one extremely important point here. We must free ourselves from the heathenish Western ideas of hell. "Hell" [Gehenna] is not an instrument of punishment created by God. That fire which is spoken of at the Last Judgment represents the love of God, and we are taught that it is the radiance of God's love which both warms and radiates and gives joy to the faithful, and burns and torments those who rejected it.[15] Those persons who in this life preferred "darkness rather than light because their deeds were evil," will, in the next life, after the resurrection, find no such darkness, but will not be able to hide from that light which they hated in this life. There, bathed in the everlasting light of God's love, which they rejected but cannot now escape, their conscience, which is like a never- dying worm, will torment them, and the passions they loved and heaped upon themselves in this life will be as serpents round about them. In other words, they will abide forever in the state they chose for themselves while still in this life. As the renowned Greek theologian Dr Alexandre Kalomiros observes:

> *This is a theme which needs to be preached with great insistence [for] not only the West but we Orthodox have departed [from it] in great numbers, causing men to fall to atheism because they are revolted against a falsified angry God full of vengeance toward His creatures...We must urgently understand that God is responsible only for everlasting life and bliss, and that hell (Gehenna) is nothing else but the rejection of this everlasting life and bliss, the everlasting revolt against the everlasting love of God. We must urgently remember and preach that it is not a creation of God but a creation [i.e., product] of our revolted liberty, that God did not create any punishing instrument that is called hell, that God never takes vengeance on His revolted creatures, that His justice has nothing to do with the legalistic `justice' of human society which punishes the wicked in order to defend itself...That our everlasting spiritual death is not inflicted on us by God, but is a spiritual suicide, everlasting because our decision to be friends or enemies of God is a completely free and everlasting decision of the free spiritual beings created by God, a decision which is respected by God eternally and absolutely.[16]*

100

We will not continue further on this subject as we have discussed it at some length in another book already.[17] It was necessary for our purposes here to demonstrate the existential nature of the Orthodox Christian understanding of the judgment and destiny of man. That our subjective freedom and the responsibility of a free conscience, concepts basic to existentialism, are both our judges and destiny is made clear by St Ephraim the Syrian who says, "....the Gehenna of the wicked consists in what they see, and it is their very separation that burns them, and their mind acts as the flame. The hidden judge which is seated in the discerning mind [i.e., their own conscience] has spoken, and has become for them the righteous judge...."

ENDNOTES:

[1]. Value and values are not Christian terms. They are secular, mercantile expressions used in philosophy to avoid the idea of "moral." We are going to use these terms nevertheless, because they are in common use in our society and have come to have a meaning which it is necessary to address. The current meaning of the words suits our purposes well enough.

[2]. cf. Maurice Merleau-Ponty, *The Primacy of Perception*, tr. J.M. Edie (Northwestern University Press, Chicago 1964) p.5

[3]. Ode 4, Troparion 5. The references are from Gn.28:12 and Rm.12:2.

[4]. The root word of noetic is *nous*, which was used by the Orthodox fathers to designate either mind, spirit, soul or intellect, and sometimes, a combination of all of them. When we speak of something being *noetic* it signifies that which is not comprehended by reason but is rather apprehended by the intellect-spirit, both of which are in the mind. This takes place within the person, not outside him and certainly not in a transcendental universe or *noetos kosmos*. The Church fathers never use the idea of *noetic* or

101

nous in a Platonistic way.

[5]. Gnostics supposed that the passions were operations of the physical body against a "spiritual body," that is, the soul, which they supposed has a "subtle body of its own" and is somehow disconnected from the body or trapped in the body as in a prison. When the fathers used the expression "subtle body," they were simply making a distinction between the created and the uncreated, not suggesting a dualism. The Orthodox Christian fathers refute every form of soul/body dualism. The body is an electro-chemical mechanism. It can conceive nothing and do nothing without being directed by the *nous* which instigates and directs all actions of the body. The body cannot "sin," rather the mind sins through the body.

[6]. Let us be more specific about the true nature of this struggle. We are struggling to give our neo-cortex — the area of reason — control over the limbic region of the brain, the area that generates all the emotions. Our reason informed by our moral conscience, especially needs to have ascendancy and control over the hypothalamus, the region that generates anger, fear, aggression, sexual desires, craving for food, sexual love (and parental love), etc. It is the hypothalamus that signals the heart to pump faster (or "race") when action is required and the muscles need more oxygen. We will discuss this in somewhat more detail in Chapter VI below.

[7]. Not that Kane originated the schemata, but he does discuss it at some length, and he is one of my favourite lecturers on modern ethics.

[8]. Scottish Empiricist David Hume (1711-1776). The term is usually rendered "sentimentalists," however many readers would connect this with saccharine nostalgia rather than to the analysis of human sentiments. For this reason, we have rendered the term "sentimentists").

[9]. "I do not want to stop at this explanation of how the Jesus Prayer can alter the brain itself. I want to suggest that the desire to know God is hardwired into the human brain. Since we are created in the image and likeness of God, our brain, as the matrix for the mind, must most certainly be programmed with mechanisms to facilitate the knowledge of God." (Deacon Lev Puhalo, Lecture on the Jesus Prayer at the University of Victoria, 1973.)

[10]. *Concise Exposition of the Orthodox Faith*, Bk.1, 12:2. The Damascene is expressing qualities relating to the likeness and image, not definitions. Other Church fathers have pointed to additional qualities and one or two have offered definitions.

[11]. We are not referring simply to public school education, but the Church school, military training and parental teaching as well as other educational experiences.

[12]. The difficulty is that these value sentiments appear to be superseded, particularly in some primitive tribes, by their opposite devalues in relation to "others," that is, those of another tribe. The holocaust has demonstrated to us that these sentiments can be fragile even in sophisticated cultures which have been informed by the Judaeo-Christian ethos.

[13]. The George Grant Reader (Sheila Grant and William Christian editors. Toronto: University of Toronto Press, 1998) p.478. Grant often used the Good as a synonym for God. He would assert that only in loving the Good could a person truly experience beauty and mystery. It is interesting that Grant became enamoured of the Orthodox Church and mentions it in his writings. Randy Peters has a section on "Loving the Good" in his paper on George Grant, *The Cat, the Wizard and the Commongood* in **The Red Tory Journal**, Vol. 1, Nr. 1.

[14]. *Homily 84.*

[15]. See St Basil the Great, *Homily on Psalms*, 28:6.

[16]. Letter reviewing our article on Icons of the Last Judgment (see Chapter 8, *The Icon as Scripture*, Synaxis Press, 1998).

[17]. *The Soul, The Body and Death* (Synaxis Press, Dewdney, B.C.) 1996

103

VI
EXISTENTIALISM AND
MODELS OF REALITY

For now we see through a glass, darkly; but then face to face: now I know in part; but then shall I know even as also I am known (1Cor.13: 12).

So long as philosophers have been speculating, they have questioned to what extent we know reality. The proposed answers have ranged from Plato's parable of the cave (we know only shadows of the ideal forms which constitute reality) to the more concrete notions of the "mechanical universe" era. Is the question, "do we know actual reality" only a tautology or is there more to it than this? Do we see things as they actually are or do we create models of them by interpreting visual images and symbols? In short, do we have a grasp on reality or do we operate within the grid of models of reality based on concepts, clues, metaphors, indoctrination, political orientation and that which a given social entity takes to be facts? How is it that we end up with models of reality? Jose Ortega refers to them as "theorems," and offers what I think is a very good explanation:

> *Theorems are imaginary figures with contours of geometric neatness. But reality never exactly coincides with theorems. And yet there is no other manner of understanding reality than to fit, as best we can, its*

104

*perpetually shifting shapes into such prefabricated molds
as our imagination produces. Theorems allow us to take
our bearings in the chaos of reality. They may even supp-
ly the means to determine the discrepancy between reality
and the cobweb of our ideas.*[1]

We are not asking these questions about reality in
a Platonistic or scholastic way. We are not asking
whether a tree is actually the thing we see in front of
us when we gaze at an oak or a maple. We are
speaking about the realities of existence, meaning and
being. Nevertheless, in order to clarify what is meant
by "models of reality," let as look at some concrete
examples.

What we see and perceive in the physical world
around us is real — it is macro level reality.[2] How we
interpret that reality and our deeper perception of it,
however, depend on the models of reality we have
formed or that have been formed within us. When I
was serving a Tlingit Indian parish in Alaska many
years ago, I was surprised by the difference in
perception between myself and an elderly native. We
were looking at a spectacular ancient Sitka spruce.
While I was commenting on its aesthetic beauty, my
acquaintance began to address the tree. "I am speaking
to its spirit," he said in response to my inquiring gaze.
The old Tlingit man perceived the tree in a rather
different manner than I did. His model of reality
placed a spirit or soul in the tree, which could

somehow be communicated with. His model of reality in this case was informed by quite ancient cultural perceptions and senses. My model of reality about trees was shaped by both my sense of aesthetics and biological science. A log grader might have added an additional dimension of reality by mentally calculating how many board feet of lumber the tree might contain.

Modern physics does not purport to give us "reality," but clearly acknowledges that it is presenting us with models of reality, expressed in the metaphor of mathematical formalisms. Let us take, for example, our perception of the universe. The more we discover about it, the more it violates not only our current models of reality, but even our ordinary reason, and causes us to think and reconsider. This is properly considered to be intellectual growth and development. Let us take a look at models of reality relating to the universe for an actual example.

Take a round, glass bowl (a small fish bowl or vase will do) and fill it with ping pong balls or marbles. As you gaze at it, contemplate three different models of the universe. Let the walls of the bowl represent the event horizon of the known universe, or even its outer, undiscovered boundaries.

1. The ping pong balls, in our contemporary standard model, must represent the galaxies in our known universe.

2. The balls are parallel universes within the infinite "limits" of a super-universe.

3. The ping pong balls or marbles represent different dimensions of reality within our known universe.

Any one, or all, of these models of reality might be true, but they do not all correspond to our present models under which we all perceive and operate. Certainly our familiar and accepted model with the galaxies of stars, solar systems, and planets held in place by gravity rather than by astral planes, moved by spiritual entities guarding imaginary toll houses, differs radically from the models of reality almost universally held in the fertile crescent a scant few thousand years ago, and still held dogmatically to some degree by the Roman Catholic Church less than five hundred years ago. Just as it has been necessary to revise and develop such models of reality about the form of the universe in the past, almost every decade now brings us to a radical reformation of such models, as Joel Davis observes:

> *We can now perceive the universe in ways undreamed of less than a century ago. As we learn more about the cosmos with these new tools that expand the range of our senses, our "internal model" of the universe inexorably changes. Our inner vision of reality grows into a new shape in response to new knowledge.*[3]

Our models of reality may give us stability, coherence and a sense of order and permanence, but they may also engrain in us some of our worst ignorance and most murderous prejudices. If we are of a rigid, brittle nature, formed more by our political orientation than by any integrity, we may be unable to adapt to the changes in our models, or even the need for completely new models of reality. This is why some religious fundamentalists so fanatically defend clear falsehood in order to keep from losing their own personal faith: their faith is predicated on and depends upon false models of reality.

As a small child, my model of reality concerning how the world came to be was a literalist understanding of the creation narrative in Genesis. The underlying principle of my model was the wilful, intelligent and planned creation of the universe by God. As I grew older, read and became educated, my model developed away from a naive literalist understanding of the origins of the universe and man. I came to perceive the Genesis narrative as a revelation about the *meaning* of creation and of human existence, not a detailed description of the process. The basic principle underlying the concept, and upon which my own models of reality in this context were constructed, never changed. In fact, the more I learned about the form and development of the universe and life on earth, the more experience I have gained, the more firmly grounded I have become in the awareness of God's consistent direction of the unfolding of the universe and His providential care for our lives.

I have viewed the evidence before me, the varied and often contradictory models of reality and, in good existentialist fashion, made a free choice from among them. In equally appropriate existentialist fashion, I might present an argument in favour of the model of reality I subscribe to with regard to the nature and existence of the universe, but would never demand that anyone else accept it. Indeed, I am quite conscious of the fact that I must remain capable of expanding, altering or even changing the model of reality I accept in this regard. The constant for me is the certainty that the universe and mankind are the intentional creation of a loving and caring God. The mechanics are not nearly so important as the meaning.

From an Orthodox Christian existentialist point of view, the glory of the creation narrative lies in the fact that it offers us concepts of meaning to our very existence itself. If offers, in fact, a concept of *existence*, something which Positivism and Kantian Rationalism and many other schools lack or even actively avoid.

If we were frozen into the given models of reality of one or another era in human history, or even of our own lifetime, then we would not only be unable to pursue the true path of Orthodoxy, we would remain unable to grow and develop in our relationship with God. We would be reduced to a moralistic self-assertion rather than a valid inner transformation, illumination and glorification. Flexibility in our models of reality requires that we acknowledge them for the transitory collection of assumptions that they are and be willing to change them, and ultimately rise above all of them as we pursue the authentic existentialist goals of the Orthodox Christian life and struggle.

One of the great problems with the scholastic approach to Christian doctrine and dogma is that it leads to an ossified fundamentalism, and this is one of the crises with many converts to the Orthodox Christian faith from Western Christianity. They are deeply penetrated with the Western legalistic notion that dogma is a concrete statement of absolute reality which has little or no existential dimension. Perhaps a more serious issue, and the root of the problem just mentioned, with Fundamentalism and its partner Scholasticism was (and still is) that they tend to substitute the truth with the "wording" or "phrasing" of the truth. There is a kind of linguistic positivism in scholastic formulations. It is as if they believe that language as a tool can actually produce "truth". However, language obviously can only "signify" the truth. By missing the difference scholasticism became trapped in reflective analysis and both it and Fundamentalism fell into the trap of a literal understanding of "authentic" sources. Attempting to find the truth of life in formulations of any kind results in trapping life in their own inflexible patterns.

This is what we often call "ideology" and we must certainly be careful to avoid understanding the faith in such a manner. The antidote to this mistake cannot be subjective individual experience, obtained in a private manner. Even faith, individual and private, can be a false guide. On this ground, one may raise an objection to experience-as-knowledge attained by individual "meditation." However, in the Church we are not alone and we are never isolated individuals. We are "in communion" with one another and with the saints, and with Christ. This "communion", this personal mode of being, can be truly implemented only in the Church. The coherence of this experience and its "authenticity" is fine-tuned by the Holy Spirit. This is, moreover, why we always look for the "consensus" of the holy fathers. This "consensus" is not just a technicality or an agreement in wording or concepts, rather it is directly related to the "coherence" brought about by the Spirit. In this sense, "coherence" can be another way of saying experience-as-knowledge. This does not mean that all individual experience, particularly the experiences encountered by studying nature or meditating upon natural things in faith, is wrong or misleading. Such experiences very often make sense and can help people in their spiritual journey. God has not left us helpless and without some guidance. We all have a compass — the image of God imprinted on our soul. I think this is what is meant by Apostle Paul when he says that those who do not know the law do according to the law by their own nature. (The law here is knowledge of the truth). However the fulfilment of knowledge and coherent experience of the faith can only be trustworthily known in the Church, where Christ is not simply reflected (as through in a mirror) but is present in person. Moreover, they read the catechism-like statements of dogma through the scholastic and fundamentalist grid that is the principle baggage they bring with them. The crisis in the West with the dogma of the Holy Trinity, for example, is a direct result of this fallacy of misplaced concreteness, to borrow Whitehead's expression. Since no one could possibly understand the essence of the Trinity, the essence of the godhead and since the energies of God could not be created, the failure to understand dogma as a model of reality rather than a concrete expression of an absolute has weakened the fabric of Christianity and shares responsibility with the general moral fascism of fundamentalist Protestantism for the asthenia of the Christian message in today's world.

An appropriate understanding of models of reality would inform us that they present metaphor and that metaphor contains an intentional inner dissonance that warns us not to literalise. It is important for us to bear in mind that models of reality in social and political life are often shaped by communal prejudices and sometimes contrived by ideologues with a desire for power. Philosophical or dialectical theology[4] is inevitably affected by these social and political models. Theology in the Orthodox sense is "revealed theology," but it still presents us with models of reality, transcendental to be sure, but not to be literalised in such a way that it becomes idolatrous. Moreover, Orthodox Christian theology, as we will discuss in detail later, does not deal with abstractions that are removed from the human condition and human experience. The dogma of the Trinity, for example, gives us a model of reality which offers an underpinning for our moral lives while resolving in purely finite human language a seeming quandary. It gives us a model but tells us nothing of the Essence of God and gives us no real understanding of "*hypostasis*" as it relates to God. On the surface, the dogma seems unapproachable, nevertheless it impacts on our moral lives with a call to knowledge and action.[5] Like the models of reality provided with all the dogmas of the faith, this one too is far from being concrete and stagnate. The dogmas are platforms from which we may make an ascent toward a more certain knowledge and understanding, by means of our experience in a moral struggle, aided by God's grace, toward the goal of *theosis*.

THE DIVINE SERVICES AS MODELS OF TRANSCENDENTAL REALITY[6]

The Liturgy is the highest form of the human story, and

its most concrete expression. (David J. Goa)[7]

The incarnation of God has seized the universe and impelled it forward toward its final destiny of transfiguration and glory.(Deacon Lev Puhalo)[8]

That in the ekonomia of the fulness of time, he might recapitulate all things in Christ, both that which is in the heavens and that which is on earth (Eph.1:10).

Reality at all levels and in every dimension is a mystery. I will not suggest that the world which we experience with our own senses is *not* reality; nevertheless, what we perceive is the *surface* of reality, which is penetrated only with great effort over time. The more deeply we penetrate into this perceived reality, the greater the mystery becomes.

The Orthodox Christian quest for meaning and the understanding of transcendental reality is not concerned with "spirituality." As the great New Testament holy prophet Saint Seraphim of Sarov has reminded us, all our efforts and learning, fasting, prayer and the divine services, and every other aspect of the Christian struggle, are aimed at the acquisition of the Holy Spirit. The indwelling of the Holy Spirit is the ultimate goal of life in this world. We work on ourselves in order to ascend by degrees through purification to illumination to glorification. While every believer may be called a "saint," those great saints of the Church who are memorialized and venerated as vital, living examples of the goal and meaning of our Christian lives, have achieved the complete indwelling of the Holy Spirit and experienced *theosis* — glorification in Christ Jesus.

With this in mind, it should be evident that the divine services, and the Liturgy in particular, are not simply formulas to guide our worship. They are that no doubt, and revealed by God for that purpose already in Old Testament times. More significantly, the divine services are also part of the process of our purification and illumination, leading us toward glorification and *theosis*.

When the Divine Liturgy in particular, and the other services in general, are celebrated by the faithful, the Holy Spirit is in the midst of the congregation; the heavenly powers join the faithful on earth and altogether, they come before the throne of our Saviour, Jesus Christ, to glorify Him and receive the grace and great holy mysteries which He has promised us. Comprehension of this, and participating in it, requires more than merely understanding the words.

The study of the structure of Orthodox divine services is not a mere technical course. It is a spiritual examination of the inner flow, the pulse and heartbeat of the Church — the Body of Christ on earth. It should bring us to an understanding of the very essence of the Gospel, for the rhythm and content of the cycles of divine services is that of the Gospel itself; it is the rhythm of the Heavenly Kingdom, the

115

expression of the harmony and unity which come with the manifestation of the reign and rule of God.[9]

Our lives flow in rhythms and cycles. Indeed, all of nature is set to rhythms and cycles, from the life cycle of individuals to the circle of the seasons, the rotations and revolutions of solar systems. The whole universe is alive with rhythm and motion, from the largest star to the lightest lepton or massless photon. There are no inanimate objects in our universe. Every stone, every block of wood, every shard of pottery is alive with motion and interaction. From the very beginning, the vitality of what we call "lifeless elements" has been profoundly creative.

Both Holy Scripture *(Prov.8:26)* and modern physics inform us that the elements which surround us and fill our universe were only formless particles with a singleness of nature in the beginning, and these subatomic particles were gifted by the Creator with a strength of action incomprehensible to us, a strength of action profoundly evident and orderly in every micro level entity of the universe today. As a result, over millions of years, they formed, from their unions, joinings and partings, a countless variety of forms and bodies so that every known element has been created simply by the addition of neutrons and protons to the nucleus of a hydrogen atom, which is the most elementary particle. Moreover, the chemistry of every element is determined by the number of electrons in the atom. Within everything that exists, deep within beyond human eyes, no matter how inanimate the object appears, there is a microcosm of the universe. Within the atoms of every material object, subatomic particles race in orbits which are kept bound together by the forces of nature. There are cycles, rhythms and, as it were, pulse in the movement and actions of the subatomic particles which fill a bar of iron or a stone along a garden path. The universe is, in fact, dimensional as Saint Maximos the Confessor observes. The dimensions of time and eternity, the visible and invisible, the finite and the infinite, the created and the uncreated all form dimensions of being but do not give rise to any concept of dualism. Such concepts of dimension indicate the transcendent and the so-called "material," but do not state whether they interpenetrate or not.[10]

Man himself is not separate from this pattern of the universe. Heart-beat, pulse, the electrochemical functions of the brain—the individual is a living system of rhythms and cycles which cannot be unrelated to the whole.

The Orthodox Church is a living organism also, and has its own rhythms of life which, in themselves, reflect the creation and serve to sanctify it. Since the Church is the Body of Christ, its rhythms and cycles are geared to the life of Christ and designed to bring spiritual harmony to all creation, for the whole universe is being redeemed together with man, as Apostle Paul says (Rm.8:18-24). This concept of the

117

Church as a living organism is difficult for those whose models of reality are shaped by Platonistic or Gnostic dualism, but for Orthodox Christians, the visible Church is the manifest reality of the Body of Christ, and not a mere shadow of some "invisible Church."[11]

It is a commonplace of existentialism that we must be free beings, able to choose between or among alternative systems, alternative concepts of meaning, alternative paths and destinations of life itself. When we undertake to make such choices, we become responsible for them.

The "worldly system" around us also has its special rhythms of life and these, in turn, affect the rhythms and cycles of our own individual bodies and lives. The hierarchical and divinely inspired rhythms and cycles of the Church are quite different than those of the materialistic, passionate, often agitated and disjointed flow of "worldly" systems.

If we are to be one with Christ, participants in Him and in the redemption which He has offered us — truly united with His Body, the Church — then our lives must be in tune with His. The orderly procession and rhythm of the cycle of Orthodox divine services is designed to bring us into such a condition. It is designed to reorient our lives, to root out and replace the worldly, passionate rhythms which penetrate us and lead our minds, souls, and bodies captive to their concepts and cycles of life. The rhythms and cycles of

Orthodox Church life are designed to transform us so that our lives move like the ticking of a clock which is geared to the life of Christ, synchronized with the life of the heavenly kingdom. People cannot grasp this great significance if they are formed with Platonistic/Gnostic dualism woven into their models of reality, rather they would have to conceive the Church in more finite and worldly terms.

It is clear that the "world" has its own system. The things of this world; the passions, ideals, desires, and goals of this world, all work together to enslave mankind, and man has truly become enslaved. Satan accomplishes this both individually and collectively by creating a spiritual void in the life of mankind, and then convincing him that this void can be filled by material possessions, shallow, often emotionally destructive entertainments, and discordant, pulsating rhythms of popular music (including "Gospel rock") which negatively affect the rhythms of body, mind, and soul, instilling carnal agitations, confusion and selfish, irrational expectations. This is the worship of the *"prince of this world" (Jn.12: 31; 14:30; 16:11)* and its liturgical cycle is served daily on television, its litanies are chanted on radio, on records, from stages and podiums. The iconography of this worship of "the prince of this world" is portrayed on billboards and in a constant flow of commercials and advertisements. This is the cycle of life which breeds avarice, malice, crime, violence, war and stunning inhumanities and a materialism which leads to the controlled mind and the desensitized heart.

The liturgical cycle of the Orthodox Church is diametrically opposite to this. It is filled with a spirit of love, peace, inner joy, and universal harmony. It flows with a spirit of transfiguration, resurrection, new life, and blessed eternity. It is a path of liberation from the bondage of passions and fear of death.

The life of the Church, and of each of its members, is set in logical cycles, each one an expansion of the preceding one. These cycles seek to pull us away from the fallen world and toward Christ, to bring the rhythms of our life into harmony with the Gospel and the life of Christ. Nevertheless, they do not seek to deprive us of freedom of will and we make our own free choices within this framework. The gradients of illumination are essentially set by our own choices, but salvation is available to everyone who enters the path, regardless of the gradient we choose.[12]

ENDNOTES:

[1]. Jose Ortega y Gassett, *Concord and Liberty*. (The Norton Library, N.Y., 1963. Tr. Helene Weyl) pp.35-36

[2]. The idea that we cannot trust our sense perception in this regard, though no longer common, comes to us largely from Plato and in particular from *The Republic*. This idea was logical in Plato's time, when we did not have physical explanations for things like, for example, refraction and waves. Place a pencil in a glass of water and, because of refraction, it appears to be no longer straight, remove it, and it again appears straight and unbroken. If you do not understand refraction, you will think that the senses just cannot be trusted. Waves, such as those that form mirages, were not understood, so

a mirage would impel you to believe that the human senses could not be trusted and that what they saw was not reality. I believe that is why Plato/Socrates felt that material objects perceived by the senses were matters of opinion while abstract forms could be objects of noetic knowledge. Sensually perceived objects were thought to be copies of Forms which existed in Plato's *kosmos noetos*.

[3]. *Alternate Realities* (Plenum Press, New York, 1997) p.96

[4]. *Dialectic and dialectical* have had different meanings at different times. It had somewhat different meanings for various schools of philosophy from Zeno to Plato and Aristotle, from the Stoics to Hegel and Kant and finally Plekhanov and Marx. Dialectical theology follows the Stoic use of the word and indicates the art of reason. Aristotle, who informed much of the Scholastic era, considered dialectic to be argument from unsubstantiated opinion. Socrates and Plato used dialectic as a method of question and answer in the process of concluding sound definitions of terms. Kant considered dialectic (which really means "the art of conversation") to be an unsound attempt at using empirical understanding beyond its proper bounds. The Socratic/Platonistic form of dialectic was used in the judicial system and also in the process of theologizing from medieval times on, but in the Middle Ages (late medieval era) the Stoic idea of dialectic as the art of reasoning dominated the concept so that dialectical theology became a process of rationalism. Dialectical theology is basically rationalism propelled by contemporary social philosophies which seeks to give new definitions to terminology and ideas presented in Scripture and religious tradition. It provides new definitions but does not necessarily arrive at "meaning" and often creates a radical breach with more ancient definitions and concepts of meaning.

[5]. For an indispensable discussion of this subject, see, for example, St Antony (Khrapovitsky's) "The Moral Idea of the Dogma of the Holy Trinity" in *The Moral Idea of the Main Dogmas of the Church* (Synaxis Press, 1976).

[6]. For a further study of the subject, see *The Spiritual and Scriptural Meaning of The Cycle of Orthodox Christian Divine Services* by Archbishop Lazar Puhalo (Synaxis Press, Dewdney, B.C., 1996)

[7]. In an informal symposium. David Goa is one of Canada's most important philosophers.

[8]. From a Nativity sermon of then Deacon Lev Puhalo (Archbishop Lazar), delivered in Victoria, B.C. in 1974.

[9]. According to Fr John Romanides (*"Church Synods and Civilisation,"* **Theologia**, Vol.63, Issue 3, July-September, 1992) the Greek expression rendered into English as "kingdom of God," is misunderstood. The correct rendering would be "rule and reign of God," and it must be understood spiritually. The reason many rulers of the Jews rejected Christ is because they misunderstood the "kingdom" to be a worldly dominion and physical kingdom. The rule and reign of God is a manifestation of Divine Love and not a manifestation of worldly power with geographical boundaries, or even with a "spiritual geography" as is sometimes imagined. This is why the "kingdom of God" can be within you if you allow the will of God to reign in your heart.

[10]. Quantum physics points to this paradox also by allowing us to discover that particles alternate between being matter and energy or, in a manner of speaking, that a particle is but a dense moment of energy moving in space and (if time exists) also in time.

[11]. The idea, common to much of Protestantism, that there is an invisible Church which is made up of true believers from every religion, rather than a visible, hierarchical, liturgical entity, was forced upon them by two factors. The first is the reality that Protestantism has never been able to give a dogmatically unified witness and that it has in the past, and still continues, to split apart into fragments. This has led Protestant philosophers to concoct a face-saving theory of an invisible Church, with the visible denominations all being pale shadows of it. Such a teaching could only be conceived in the presence of Platonistic/Gnostic dualism. This kind of dualism is also necessary to support the heresy of Ecumenism.

[12]. We could continue, speaking of icons and the Orthodox Church architecture, but these have been written about often enough. We will refer the reader to *The Icon as Scripture* (Synaxis Press, 1999).

VI
LIVING THEOLOGY
the Existential Nature of Orthodox Theology

1
PREFACE

Let us say simply that theology was originally a form of response to challenges to Apostolic doctrine. In particular, early theology explained and defended the elements that were incorporated to form the Symbol of Faith ("creed") and framed the Apostolic understanding of the Gospels, in a pattern and matrix borrowed from philosophy. In short, this theology clarified elements of Apostolic revelation for the sake of the faithful, and was used to formulate the Symbol of Faith. The earliest manifestations of our theology appear in the letters of Apostle Paul, the *Didascalion*, the Gospel of John and the letters of St Ignatios "the God-bearer."[1]

The supreme expression of Orthodox Christian theology is, however, liturgical. Our theology is expressed primarily in our communal worship, in which we not only worship our Saviour, but also learn to fulfil His moral imperatives to love one another as He loved us, to have empathy for one another (love your neighbour as yourself) and not to demand our own, but to be humble before others. In the congregation, if we are serious minded, we can develop skill in bridling our ego and learn to grow in unselfish love for our neighbour. Such growth, understanding and self-control are in the very foundations of any living theology. Our theology should offer us an underpinning for this moral/theological struggle, just as the Liturgical cycle does. This is at the root of a vital, living and existential theology.

The divine liturgy, vespers and matins services, especially those for the Sunday worship cycle and the twelve great feastdays, provide the faithful with out deepest and most transforming theological experiences.

In this latter sense, the theology of the Church unfolds in communal, liturgical worship that brings us not only before God, but into the presence of neighbours in a common, communal action. The theology expressed in our liturgical cycle is a living experience that offers us a guide toward the acquisition of the indwelling Holy Spirit, and toward a true life in Christ. The hymns and readings in the divine services all provide us with solid theology.

My mentor, the late Father John Romanides, has reminded us that theology will not suffice to bring us to purification, illumination and glorification. It can only set boundaries to help keep us on the path of inner transformation, to guide us from falling into error and losing our way.

It is unfortunate that later theology became more of a religious philosophy that could lead, on the one hand, to a fundamentalist ossification and descend into a dry moralism in which mere obedience and formulae for external behaviour replaced the struggle for the transformation of the inner person. To the degree that we grow in a sincere, unselfish love, we defeat the power of Satan and the darker inclinations within our own inner persons and and in our congregations. This is what it means to actually live the theology we hold.

Such "school" theology becomes rigid, loses its spiritual vitality and serves more as a yoke of lifeless obedience and a regulation of external behaviour, rather than an aid to our inner transformation. On the other hand, movements such as Sofianism and Telonism have taken theology into the realm of wild and unsober speculations and ideologies.

A vital and living theology should be an underpinning for our daily moral struggle and be a wellspring that develops a mindset that leads to our inner transformation, to a genuine and sincere life in Christ. The theology expressed in our liturgical cycle is the richest and most transforming source for us if and when we strive to actually practise that illumination in the manner described above. This is a foundation that can lead us to do naturally, not by compulsion, but from love, those things that pertain to a true moral life. A theology which does not provide this foundation and lead us in this direction is not altogether useful.

What first attracted me to Father John Romanides back in 1956 or 57 was an article of his titled *The Nature of Man According to the Divine Services.*[2] It opened my heart to the study of the contents of the divine services, though only some years later were they fully available in English. The liturgical cycle became my primary source for the vital theology of Orthodox Christianity.

Allow me to suggest that the Divine Service cycle still forms the best source of our theology, totally consistent with the holy father. It provides us, in a more vivid form that is both heard and experienced in the act of unity of worship with out brothers and sister---our primary neighbours---an entrance into the living theology of a dynamic, vital, living faith in the Living God.

MORE DETAILED DISCUSSION

Theology exists in more than one register, however, and we must discuss it in this broader sense. In the first register, Orthodox theology is expressed in the relationship of the faithful with God, made possible by Christ Jesus. In this register, our theology is unchanging and examines only better and more comprehensive ways of explaining the elements of the Symbol of Faith in a more expansive way. At another level, Orthodox Christian theology explores the life of man, including his spiritual life. Here, it must engage the contemporary life of man, encountering new knowledge and understanding which arises with scientific and medical advances in each epoch. Our theology must examine all this in relation to the dogmas and teachings of the faith without any fear of accepting new understandings which have been proved to be true, in relation to the teachings of the holy fathers. To shun or deny newly discovered truths about the universe, about the earth, and the more complete understanding of the nature of man is to reduce the faith to a blind ideology defended with falsehood and fraud. Truth and reality are not enemies; and reality and faith are not mutually exclusive.

Ultimately, nevertheless, Orthodox Christian theology must be lived to be authentic. Otherwise, it consists only in fine and lofty words that have no particular substance.

If theology is presented primarily as a series of theoretical philosophical posits or concepts, or a collection of theoretical "definitions," then it is worth no more than any other system of philosophy. Theology, literally understood, may mean "knowledge of (or about) God," but God can only be known in a living experience with God. Such a "knowing" and such an experience are possible only through Christ Jesus. Whether one understands the meaning of the Uncreated Energy of God or not is no hindrance to living the theology of the heart, the theology of Liturgy and Communion. Head knowledge is gradually transformed into heart knowledge largely through worship.

We know God by means of revelation. The more profound question about Orthodox theology, then, is how revelation is received and how is it verified. We will examine this a little at a time as our discussion unfolds.

The dogmas of the Orthodox faith are not derived from philosophical deliberations, but the responses to challenges to the dogmas are necessarily expressed using the structure of philosophy, and borrowing language from it. Philosophy itself is a major aspect of the great human dialogue, and through it, we can gain knowledge and understanding. This is why its structure and much terminology have been borrowed from it for the purpose of explicating the dogmas of the faith. Ultimately, "theology," as it is usually understood, is not about "knowing God," but about explaining the revelation that has been given through the Church, as Paul says: "....to enlighten all as to what is the ekonomia of the mystery which had been hidden in God from all ages; [Him] Who created all things through Jesus Christ, in order that the manifold wisdom of God might now be revealed through the Church....(Eph.3:9-10). We learn something *about* God from theology in this register, though we also learn that we cannot *know* God from it.[3] Knowing Him takes place in the heart, through "heart theology."

Dogma is based in revelation and is unchanging. It is arrived at by *theoria*, and to the greatest degree possible expressed, as well as we are able, in human languages in a form we call theology. Still, theology, in Orthodox Christian terms, exists, as we indicated, in two registers. *Theoria* (in the Orthodox sense[4]) is true theology, revealed theology. In a different register, philosophical theology seeks to express more clearly the dogmatic teachings of the faith in response to challenges to the Apostolic Tradition. This theology does not seek to create new teachings or alter dogma, rather it seeks to clarify it, not in a manner frozen in time, but in terms of each generation with its new knowledge, more accurate scientific understandings, advances in medicine, changes in language and the meanings of words[5] etc. Each new epoch holds particular challenges to the faith, and must be responded to in their own time and place.

To be meaningful and successfully convey the faith, theology cannot be static or petrified. When new knowledge in any field has been discerned and proved, to deny that knowledge would be not only to lie, but to demonstrate one's own doubts about the faith itself. Orthodox theology must deal only in truth, and what is thought to be true in one epoch is often proved, in a later epoch, to be untrue. Our medical and biological knowledge, our cosmology, history and knowledge of physiology and neuroscience (the manner in which the brain operates), and many other fields of knowledge, have all changed dramatically, especially in the past two hundred years. It is necessary for us to find ways to explain the dogmas of the faith – and here we refer primarily to the things expressed in the Symbol of Faith ("creed") — must be expressed in relation to the contemporary state of knowledge.

There is yet another register in which theology exists, and this latter register is of interest in this discussion. This expression of our theology is aimed primarily at offering moral guidance in each unfolding epoch, with its enhanced information and knowledge. We have emphasised that Orthodox Christian theology is existential; this means that it applies to the realities of our daily lives and struggles, while leaving us with the freedom to take responsibility for our own lives.. In this register, we will also speak about a "living theology." If, as Saint Antony Khrapovitsky asserts, the dogmas of the faith do not underpin our daily moral struggle, if they do not have a "moral idea" or ideal that informs our own daily struggle and spiritual aspirations, then there is not much point in them having been revealed to us. The expressed dogmas of Orthodox Christianity are not metaphysical abstractions, but rather impart to us a path to living with real and attainable spiritual aspirations.

While all our dogma is concisely expressed in the Symbol of Faith,[6] and remains unchanging, this does not mean that the Orthodox Church and its theology is stagnate and unable to embrace new knowledge and understanding when it is proved to be true. Science is continuously presenting us with such new knowledge and understandings. Since Orthodox Christian theology is existential in nature, it is not frozen in abstractions and ideologies, but guides us into our encounter with this new knowledge and helps shape the way we deal with it. Even the concepts of physical reality change over time, and a truly living theology leads us through such changes. All authentic theology serves for the underpinning of our actual, daily moral struggle – our struggle in real-time, in life itself.

Scholastic and other Western systems of theological philosophy are not adequate for the expression of Orthodox Christian theology. The renowned Western theologian Karl Rahner gives a fairly accurate assessment of the general basis of this spiritual/theological difference in these words:

> *The East thought in terms of a dynamic saving history and an ascending order of things, beginning with the economy of the Trinity and closely bound up with soteriology.... Redemption is regarded in the East as a real ontological process that begins with the incarnation, discloses the immanent economy of the Trinity, ends with the divinization [theosis] of the world and first proves its triumph in Christ's Resurrection....in contrast, Western theology regards the incarnation of The Logos almost exclusively as the means of constituting a fit agent capable of making satisfaction for sin. Though aware of the divinization [theosis] of the world, it lays much more stress on Christ's atonement for sin on the Cross and on forgiveness.[7]*

Rahner in correct in referring to the Orthodox Christian concept of a dynamic saving history and of our concept of redemption as a real ontological process. Redemption, our salvation, is not found in a static notion of a substitutionary human sacrifice that took place more than 2000 years ago. Rather, it is life-long process for each of us; a process of purification, illumination and glorification that is guided by the highest form of our theology.

The Western version of the Judaeo-Christian tradition is really built largely upon the old Latin legal ideal — hence the doctrines of Original Sin, retributive justice[8] and the human sacrifice Atonement or Juridical Justification theory of salvation, considered to be serious errors by the Orthodox Christian Church — and upon the teachings of the neo-Platonist philosopher Augustine of Hippo, and the Scholastic system which was built upon both these teachings and Aristotelian rationalism. In fact, the late Greek theologian, Fr John Romanides, sorrowfully remarks:

> *Beyond any doubt the most ironic tragedy in history is that Western theologians, and finally an illusionist papacy turned Augustine's endeavour into an infallible accomplishment and brought about the final touches of a separation which was long in the making.*[9]

In the West, one can speak of an "Apostolic-

Patristic Age" in the past tense because the apostolic-patristic tradition was replaced there by the legacy of the Dark Ages and the era of Scholasticism. There, the great Orthodox Church fathers, such as Sts Cyprian of Carthage, Hilary of Poitiers, Germain of Auxerre, Hilary of Arles, John Cassian, Lupe of Troyes and Irenae of Lyons, were eclipsed by the new school men and Aristotelian Rationalism and nominalism.[10] In this new era of Western philosophical theology, the laws and ideals of the medieval duel and feudalism were adapted into the "satisfaction" theory of salvation, and the concept of the relationship between God and man was reshaped by a number of factors, renaissance humanism and the industrial revolution cult of the ego, among them..[11]

In the Orthodox Christian East, one cannot speak of a separate "Apostolic-Patristic Age," because the Orthodox Church has never ceased to live in that tradition. We find, therefore, a clear and easily visible line of great Church fathers, from Apostle Paul, Sts Polikarp of Smyrna, Ignatios the Godbearer, through Sts Basil the Great, Irenae of Lyons, John Chrysostom, to St Symeon the New Theologian in the 11th century, St Gregory Palamas in the 14th century, to Sts Paissy Velichkovsky and Sts Antony the Metropolitan of Kiev and Justin the New of Serbia in the 20th century. Among these fathers one finds a consensus that is always consistent with the Apostolic fathers and their era. As a matter of fact, we should note that in the Orthodox Christian Church there is no "theological system," no scholastically systematized body of expressed theological theory as, for example, the *Summa Theologica*. Only one of the earlier fathers, St John the Damascene, even set down in outline form an exposition of the basic teachings of the Church. Such a systematized theology would be an anomoly for the Orthodox Christian Church, because it would contradict the apostolic-patristic spirit and tradition, which never sought to rationalize the gospel or reduce theology to a legalistic code of systematic philosophy of definitions. The theology of the dogmas of the faith has not been a theoretical development in the East. It has arisen for the purpose of clarifying the Apostolic doctrine and state the already existing dogmatic revelation for the purpose of responding to challenges raised against them.

The fathers have always "theologized" in precisely the same manner and in exactly the same spirit as the apostles Wrote their letters (Epistles). Neither the apostles nor the evangelists ever decided at one or another time to "sit down and write a Bible," nor did any one of them claim that he had been given a special "call" or "commission" to take up pen and write some "holy scripture." Indeed, the apostles and evangelists were never in any great hurry to write any-thing. The Gospels were written decades after the Resurrection, and then primarily as responses to false writing that sought to pre-empt Christ's ministry. The Gospels of Matthew, Mark and Luke were not written by actual apostles, and were received by the Church without any specific attribution, except for Luke. Their intention was not to "write a bible," but to record the traditions that they had heard from the Apostles.

When they did write, it was primarily in the form of letters addressed to specific problems or questions which had arisen. In other words, they did not write for the purpose of establishing a "Bible," but rather to preserve the unity of the faith in sound doctrine and defending the unity and uniqueness of the Holy Church. They gave nothing new, but only drew from what was already there in the Sacred Tradition of the Church, maintained by the Holy Spirit. Thus, for example, Luke wrote not a book of the gospel, but a letter to Theophilus, expressing for him the life of Christ and its meaning and significance as contained in Sacred Tradition – the Tradition that he received from the disciples who had walked with Christ. John, whose version of the gospel is very theological indeed, wrote it nearly a hundred years after the incarnation of God, and he wrote it only upon the entreaties of the presbyters of the churches in Asia Minor. Paul wrote to the Galatians not to establish some Divine Scripture, but to explain correct doctrine to them against a false teaching which contradicted the First General Council — the Apostolic Council of Jerusalem. And James wrote his Epistle, not trying to contribute to the writing of a Bible, but to correct the false teachings of those who had misrepresented Paul's words about salvation by faith without works. Yet, all these letters expressed the doctrines of the faith which the apostles had received from Christ, and which were and are woven into the very fabric and practice and being of the Orthodox Church. These doctrines were not "developed," but were given a direct expression only when necessary to combat a heresy which undermined our salvation and the need arose, and to preserve the unity and uniqueness of the Church and a more clear understanding of the ministry of Christ.. Indeed, the Orthodox Church, when it was establishing and creating the Bible, did not accept everything that was written by every apostle as being "Scripture." Some were only histories, and there were also apocryphal works, contrived by various Gnostic sects in order to delude the faithful. As a matter of fact, it was precisely because of these contrived, false gospels that the Holy Orthodox Church felt compelled, for the safety of the faithful, to create the Bible.

The fathers dogmatized in precisely the same manner. Just as Paul had to expound sound doctrine against the Gnostic heresies in Corinth for the sake of the gospel of salvation, so also the early fathers, gathered in the ancient councils, had to give more precise and detailed form to the dogmas of the faith in order to preserve the faithful from other heresies. The dogmas were not acts of legislation, but clear pronouncements of the gospel revelation, around which all believers could gather as a visible point of unity of faith. No one invented or contrived doctrines, dogmas or teachings. They were always present in the Church as the "Apostolic Rule of Faith," and one could suggest that the first example of New Testament Scripture is the Divine Liturgy itself, established by Apostle James.[12] When, however, the revelation and apostolic tradition were challenged, they had to be set forth in more precise expressions for the sake of the faithful.

Neither the apostles, evangelists nor the fathers of the Church have been concerned with abstract metaphysics, or speculative or dialectical theology. Their theology has always been existential in the *true* meaning of the word; that is, Orthodox theology is practical, being expressed in life itself. Man has free will and bears responsibility for his personal decisions and commitments. He may choose to accept or reject the cooperation of God's grace in the shaping of his life. This is the primary concern of theology: the "working out of one's own salvation with fear and trembling" (Phil.2:12), as Apostle Paul instructs us. Theology is not only "knowledge about God," it is also concerned with knowledge about humanity. Please note that we referred to "knowledge," not "ideology."

2
ASCETICISM
(SPIRITUAL STRUGGLE):
EXISTENTIALISM IN PRACTICE

*Platonistic mysticism was the cause of the
collapse of sound Orthodox theology in
Russia from the 17th century to the present.* Rt Rev Ierotheos Vlakhos

Theology exists in more than one register. In the
first register, Orthodox theology is expressed in
the relationship of the faithful with God, made
possible by Christ Jesus. In this register, our theology
is unchanging and examines only better and more
comprehensive ways of explaining the elements of the
Symbol of Faith in a more expansive way. At another
evel, Orthodox Christian theology explores the life of
man, including his spiritual life. Here, it must engage
the contemporary life of man, encountering new
knowledge and understanding which arises with
scientific and medical advances in each epoch. Our
theology must examine all this in relation to the
dogmas and teachings of the faith without any fear of
accepting new understandings which have been
proved to be true, in relation to the teachings of the
holy fathers.

To shun or deny newly discovered truths about
the universe, about the earth, and the more complete

understanding of the nature of man is to reduce the faith to a blind ideology defended with falsehood and fraud. Truth and reality are not enemies; and truth and faith are not mutually exclusive.

Ultimately, however, Orthodox Christian theology must be lived to be authentic. Otherwise, it consists only in fine and lofty words that have no substance.

In some quarters, what is considered to be *spiritual* life has been perverted into either mysticism or a pietistic "spirituality." In such thought, mysticism and spirituality are sometimes seen in opposition to theology. In such instances, theology is often seen as external to, and separate from, spiritual endeavour *[podvig; askesis]*, or even a hindrance to it.[13] In the absence of a vital, living theology, mysticism in particular (and "spirituality" in general), though contradictory to any sound theology, naturally attracted those who desired something more than dry philosophy or simple emotionalism. This is, perhaps, why so many people who reject "organised religion" prefer to refer to themselves as "spiritual but not religious." Mysticism, and the concept of pietistic spirituality that develops from it, is a subjective emotional endeavour that leads inevitably to spiritual delusion and error. "Spirituality," whether in the modern or antique context is expressed either as *spiritualism* or as a less intense form of mysticism.

ASCETICISM
Existentialism or Platonism?

139

Spiritual Struggle versus Mysticism.
Spirituality or the Indwelling of the Holy Spirit?

The true goal of our Christian life is the acquisi-
tion of the Holy Spirit. Fasting, vigils, prayer, charity
and all good deeds done for the sake of Christ are but
means for the acquisition of the Holy Spirit. (St
Seraphim of Sarov.)[14]

By the late 1700's, Platonistic and Gnostic dualism had corrupted Orthodox Christian thought and understanding in Russia as it had in the West centuries before. Russian theology began its 300 year "Latin Captivity." One of the main culprits in this corruption of Orthodox thought was the introduction of Augustine of Hippo's theology. The same corruption would take place in Greece a little later and the strongly anti-dualistic teachings of the holy fathers would be almost completely discounted, as they are today is some Orthodox jurisdictions.[15]

From an Orthodox Christian perspective, we are not seeking "spirituality," rather we are seeking the indwelling of the Holy Spirit. Both pietistic spirituality and mysticism are erroneous in every context. Spiritual struggle (or "asceticism," which constitutes the normal Orthodox Christian approach to life) has nothing to do with mysticism,[16] pietism or self-inflicted suffering. Moreover, it is false to presume that asceticism is the realm of monastics or a rarefied few in the Orthodox Christian Church. Asceticism is the norm of life for all right-believing Orthodox Christians. The much misunderstood term "asceticism" means "training" and, perhaps, exercising virtue to strengthen it. It certainly means to struggle to have self-control and self-discipline.

Theology without asceticism (spiritual struggle) is dead legalism, while spiritual struggle (asceticism) without sound theology is sheer mysticism and delusion. It is this bond of sound theology and asceticism (spiritual struggle) which comprises the Orthodox Christian spiritual life, for it pertains to body and soul together as a unified organism and constitutes the "living theology of Orthodox Christianity."[17] The Orthodox Christian spiritual life of measured asceticism is as totally inseparable from the dogmas and theology of the faith as these dogmas and theology are inseparable from the gospel of salvation itself. Indeed, as the great 20th century father of the Church, Saint Antony, Metropolitan of Kiev, has demonstrated, the very moral life of Christianity, which leads to salvation, rests upon the truths of the inseparable dogmas of the Trinity, the Holy Church, the Incarnation, Redemption and the Holy Spirit.[18] Thus we cannot speak of Orthodox Christian spiritual life without speaking of the dogmas and theology of the faith. Nor could we express our meaning of the term "living theology" without first laying down these sketchy presuppositions concerning the Orthodox spiritual mind.

The Orthodox Christian life is a wholly creative,

progressive existence which, in Lossky's words, is a *"renunciation of, and moving away from, all that is fixed and stagnant, and reaching out toward the final consummation,"*[19] toward what is perfect, complete and eternal. It is impossible to discuss or to apprehend this creative progression in terms of non-Orthodox philosophy or philosophical concepts, for they themselves are merely human systems of thought, caught in the realm of creatureliness, unable to contemplate anything else except things like themselves — that is, things finite and created.

The theology of Orthodoxy, then, is a living, creative force precisely because it is inseparably bound up with the mystical-ascetical[20] life — that is, with the very real struggle actually and fully to live the theology. Whereas, among some scholars, an individual theological writer strives to be creative by giving new forms and expression to philosophical theology, in Orthodoxy every single practising Orthodox Christian progresses corporately in the Church by yielding to the creative power of the Holy Spirit, and allowing divine theology to give new forms and expression to his own being. In some systems, creativity in theology consists in only a dialectical exercise; in Orthodox Christianity, it is a transfiguration and deification of the entire, unified being of the individual. This is most clearly expressed in the respective concepts of salvation. In Western Christianity, salvation is viewed almost exclusively as a legal process, a punitive event carried out between a vengeful father figure and a dutiful son.

In Orthodox Christianity, salvation is realized as a living, vital process,[21] one in which the response of man to the co-suffering love of Christ leads to illumination and purification and, ultimately, to glorification and theosis.[22]

Asceticism (spiritual struggle) is an expression which faces the semantic wall. For the Orthodox it means something essentially very different from what it may mean to a non-Orthodox person. Indeed, to a purely superficial viewer, all asceticism appears generally identical and is often identified as either self-affliction and/or sheer mysticism. This external, apparent sameness comes from the fact that deity is incomprehensible. Even the concept of deity is above ordinary human reason. This is why St Gregory the Theologian says that *"Every concept of God is merely a simulacrum, a false likeness, an idol: it cannot reveal God Himself."*[23]

In a certain sense, what separates ascetic spiritual struggle from materialistic rationalism is the acceptance or rejection of the incomprehensibility, the wholly "otherness" of God. In any society that does not worship matter and the human ego, in the absence of revelation or a sound theology, a religion based in mysticism is likely to grow up simply because of the natural longing of the human soul to seek its source. Often, the striving toward the divine is manifested in excessive self-abnegation and an introspective mysticism which assumes that the spirit of man can develop and ascend independently of the body. In

Gnostic and oriental forms, there is a concept that the material and immaterial parts of man are at enmity with one another, and that the "spirit" (or "soul") must escape the material (the body) in order to experience spiritual ascent.

All mankind is born with the grace to know that God exists and, also, with the grace to know that one must seek God. Hence, the soul, which realizes the incomprehensibility of deity, will be led to either mysticism or, in the presence of a sound, living theology, to controlled spiritual struggle as a way toward the deity, knowing the limits of human reason.

Orthodoxy, however, is sharply different from all religions based in mysticism;[24] first, because God has become incarnate and revealed Himself to us; second, because the incarnation of God and the possession by Christ of both natures (divine and human) has made possible what was previously impossible: it has reconciled the material with the immaterial in a certain way and has shown us that physical, material things can be grace-bearing.

Above all, it brought the heavenly Church to earth, rescued the earthly Church and restored it to oneness with the heavenly. This single unity of heavenly and earthly is the essential meaning of Orthodoxy. It is what makes Orthodox Christian spiritual struggle a practical reality — a sort of response or yielding to the magnetic force of divine love, which draws the believer to a desire for a knowledge of God, not the merely descriptive knowledge of written teachings, nor the egoistic subjective emotionalism of mysticism or Christian enthusiasm cults, but the knowledge of first-hand experience. God communes with us through His uncreated energy; we respond with our created energy. We have a close, personal relationship with God in this manner, through divine grace.

Theology, then, because it indicates "knowledge about God," is a spiritual process which is guided and guarded by certain dogmas, doctrines and Scripture. It is true theology and true spiritual struggle (asceticism) because it takes place within the Holy Church, the Head of which is the object of all theological and spiritual strivings.

Nevertheless, no expanse of definition will completely explain the meaning of "asceticism" (spiritual struggle), for all definition is essentially scholastic and legalistic. We can, however, give this elementary explanation; asceticism is the spiritual basis of the life of every Orthodox believer and is manifested as the spiritual struggle which touches each and every truly Orthodox person. It is essentially the struggle to acquire the indwelling of the Holy Spirit, which can lead us to a true unselfish love, and lead us on the path to a genuine co-suffering love taught by Christ and by the dogmas of the Orthodox Church. The Orthodox Christian concept of morality is far removed from those notions of legalistic norms of "good behaviour," which curse and condemn those who fall below a certain minimum level of "acceptable" conduct.

The concept of morality which permeates Orthodox Christian theology is an ideal of active struggle with one's own weaknesses and vices, and a gradual transformation and transfiguration of the entire being of the individual: purification, illumination and glorification.[25] This cannot be accomplished without an ascent in unselfish love.

In this respect asceticism may be defined in existentialist terms as: in striving to live the teachings of Christ, in obedience to His Church, one attains grace from God. Ascending by means of this grace, one *experiences* the reality of the theology. So, at this level, we can see the two inseparable phenomena of theology and asceticism thus: asceticism (spiritual struggle) is the means by which one strives to *live* the theology and to *experience* the reality of the theology.

3
THE NECESSITY OF THEOLOGY
AND ASCETICISM (SPIRITUAL STRUGGLE)

Why are theology, spiritual struggle, asceticism, dogmas and doctrines necessary? Because of the fall of man; because our first ancestors introduced the ontological principle of alienation and separation from God (the actual meaning of "sin") into the symmetry of the cosmos, and most specifically into the common human nature.

When we speak of a "fallen human nature," we

mean primarily a proclivity to habitually misuse our energies, with the cumulative corrupting influence that this implies. The healing of the fallen nature consists in the struggle for the proper use of our energies. The goal is to restore man to his original vocation. This is the existential struggle to recover our full responsibility for our lives and reclaim an authenticity of life.

Humanity was created in God's image and likeness. We understand that "image" refers to free will and intellect, while "likeness" refers to the virtue of selfless love. We can phrase this in a more complex but more complete and accurate manner by saying that the image of Christ in us is what makes us human. No matter how darkened and distorted that image may become in us, man, even in his fallen state, is still ontologically the image of God. The image of God is the seal of Christ upon all humanity, while the likeness is the free acquisition of the divine *Energy* into our hearts and minds. In the truly natural human state, this likeness and image are in complete harmony, working to bring man upward toward perfection in God.

The fallen (sub-natural) state in which man now lives is a condition of internal disharmony and dissonance, of two internal factions warring against one another. In such a condition, progress toward knowledge, perfection and an internal unity of the "image" and "likeness" is really not possible, a fact self-evident in man's scientific-philosophical progress. For, by means of such progress, man has both made magnificent strides and great achievements, while at the same time making the earth practically unliveable and rapidly progressing toward destroying all life on earth. He has advanced in these contradictory and mutually opposed directions because he either denies or ignores the dissonance of fallen nature and the irrationality of fallen humanity's intellectual faculties. The "image" cannot function in an unperverted manner while it remains in disharmony with the "likeness" — that is, man cannot think, reason or exercise his free will in a completely rational, undestructive manner while he has not yet restored his reason and will to harmony with the likeness of the virtue of selfless love.

The fall was a true descent, a turning away from God, a separation from God and His life-giving grace. Man's fallen state is a fact, and thus Orthodoxy concerns itself with the restoration of human nature to its natural harmony, with how man might be healed so that his faculties function normally. The means by which this can be achieved is seen to be the moral struggle against all barricades to selfless love and to the realization of true harmony; that is the experiencing of a unity of love with God. Essentially, Orthodox Christian theology presents an ascetical world-view because theology is useful only when man is struggling to actually live it in a very real sense, and he can live it only if he first comes to grips with the passions that have formed a barricade on his path. We have already cited Apostle Paul's teaching about the two opposing forces at work within man. Orthodox Christian asceticism represents the ongoing expression of a commitment to the positive, moral force, while also expressing man's active struggle against the negative, sinful force.

True theology is not, and cannot be, simply a system of religious philosophy, a set of expressed beliefs or a collection of doctrines and dogmas which are "accepted" in order to be saved or to know God, nor can it be merely the explanation or clarification of a faith or system of teachings. Man himself is a theological creature and all true theology must be as alive, vivid, creative and active as man is himself. The Orthodox Christian is called to struggle to ascend beyond this written or expressed theology — to a point where dogmas and doctrines are no longer necessary, no longer of any use — to a point at which the living experience of mutual love between God and man shows all dogma and doctrine to have been no more than a framework of truth which was but a hint and shadow of reality.

Orthodox theology reflects the reality of God and the heavenly kingdom because the Orthodox Church is, in fact, the kingdom of God manifested on earth.[26] The Church is One — both on earth and in heaven. In the earthly facet of the Church we have the reflection: we see, as Apostle Paul says, "as in a mirror darkly;" in the heavenly, we have the reality: there we see, in the Apostle's words, "face to face." In the Church on earth, the expressed theology teaches us as much of reality as we are able to bear, "Now I know in part." In the heavenly, we shall experience the reality, "but then shall I know even as I am known," the Apostle concludes.[27] As the Church is One, it bears the reality, both of heaven and earth, but reveals that reality to each Orthodox Christian to the extent that the individual is able to receive and bear it. And how does one become able to receive and bear that revelation? By struggling to live the theology of the Church, to fulfil in obedience what *She* teaches us to fulfil, or rather, what the Holy Spirit has revealed to us through Her. In this manner we prepare the soul to receive the Holy Spirit, which imparts all knowledge. It is *nothing* to agree with or even to adopt the whole of Orthodox Christian written theological texts, for one will not yet be Orthodox, not yet agree with or possess the truth, nor be able to gain entrance into the heavenly kingdom. The gate to the heavenly Church is the earthly Church, and Orthodox theology is the staircase from the basement to the top floor. Remove a staircase from within its house, and no matter how much you climb it, you will never ascend to the top floor. On the other hand, if you leave the staircase within its house but refuse to climb it, you will still not ascend to the top floor.

It would be very wrong to think that theology consists of a written code or formulation of religious beliefs. "Theology" indicates "knowledge about God,"[28] and God cannot be known from a code, creed or formula, or even from an explanation of them. God can be known only from a living experience and, therefore, theology has more than one level. We see it first of all as a collection of revealed information, which tells us what to believe and what not to believe about God and our relationship with Him. In other words, we encounter theology first of all rather as a border or boundary, a "safety net" as it were, which not only guides but also protects our spiritual advance to the profound depths of divine theology. If we stay within that boundary we do not enter into falsehood, nor fall into heresy. Orthodox theology, however, reveals much more than what is knowable and unknowable about God: it also reveals how to be saved and how to ascend to a knowledge of God founded on an actual experience of God. As the beginning of salvation and of the knowledge of God is faith in Jesus Christ, we must first understand what is meant by faith. The mystery of faith is also the basis of Orthodox Christian theology, with its ascetical ascent.

Before discussing the meaning of faith, let us summarize what we have said so far about the spiritual theology of Orthodoxy, let us turn to the works of St Gregory of Nyssa, and more precisely to his work, *On the Life of the Prophet Moses*. Here we read:

> *I think this idea quite fills all that we have already said. When God speaks of a place, He does not mean a space which can be quantitatively measured...but rather by using the analogy of a measurable*

*surface, He is guiding the reader to a reality which is
infinite and without limit.*

And further, St Gregory says:

> *Seeing that you have stretched forth that which
> is before you with a great desire, and you never experi-
> ence complete satiation in your progress, nor are you
> aware of any limit to the good, as your longing calls
> you on to ever more and more: here is a place .. .that
> is so vast that he who runs in it will never be able to
> reach the end of his course. And yet from another
> point of view, this course has stability; for God said,
> `I will set you on the rock' (Ex.33:22). But here we
> have a very great paradox: motion and stability are
> identical. For usually speaking, one who is rising is
> not standing still, and the one who is standing still is
> not rising. But here, one arises precisely because he is
> stationary ....*[29]

Thus, we have the revealed dogmas of the faith,
the Orthodox teachings and explanations of the
Divine Scripture. These constitute the written or
expressed theology of the Holy Church, and are a rock
of truth and stability. If we stand firmly, immovably
upon this rock by means of spiritual struggle,
obedience and the ascetical purification of the heart
and soul, we can ascend upward until we experience
the reality of what the dogmas teach. Orthodox
asceticism — mystical theology in our present context

— is, simply stated: to live and fulfil the moral struggle which leads to salvation, and to experience with the whole being that which cannot be understood by our fallen intellects and reasons.

4
THE MEANING OF FAITH

Faith is an existential experience, an orientation responsibly chosen, not a legal agreement between God and the believer for mutual recognition of each other's existence.

One of the most misrepresented teachings of Scripture — and I think that it is often wilfully misrepresented — is the teaching about salvation by faith. In general, Western theology considers the matter of salvation as an incident in history: Christ bleeding on the Cross, which is why blood and agony are so important in many Western pictures of the crucifixion. We are not saved by Christ's death alone, but also by His life,[30] and we are not saved by belief in an incident in history, but by living faith in an actual Life — a Divine-human Life, and faith in all that this Life taught us.

The New Testament teaching about salvation by grace through faith is the very foundation of the theology of Orthodox Christianity. The whole life of prayer, fasting and struggle common to all Orthodox people is nothing else but the manifestation of gospel faith. This point is beautifully made by Fr Michael Pomozansky, late professor of Dogmatics at Holy Trinity Seminary. In his textbook on dogmatic theology, he says:

> *The history of Christ's Church is filled with miracles of saints in all centuries. It is not, however, faith in general, but true Christian faith which works miracles. Faith is effective not by the power of imagination, nor by self-hypnosis, but by the fact that it unites one with the source of all life and power — with God. It is a vessel with which water is scooped up; but one must be at this water and lower the vessel into it; this water is God's grace ....Thus, it is difficult to give a definition of what faith is. When the apostle says, `Faith is the assurance of things hoped for, the evidence of things not seen' (Hb.11: 1), he does not touch upon the nature of faith, but only upon the object of its gaze — upon what is expected, upon the unseen, and it shows precisely that faith is a penetration by the soul into the future (the `things hoped for') and into the invisible (the reality of `things unseen'). This gives testimony of the mystical nature of faith.*[31]

St Antony, Metropolitan of Kiev, reminds us that the term "faith" or "to believe" is used in a number of different senses in Scripture,[32] so that if one passage, written from the Holy Spirit, tells us that we are made righteous by faith without works of the law, and another, also from the Holy Spirit, tells us that faith without works cannot save us, then both are speaking the truth. They are simply using the terms "faith" and "works" in different contexts. Law cannot save us because it has no power to work an inner transformation of the human heart; it can only coerce correct behaviour (which in itself is only a human work which all are capable of). It can also deprive us of a full personal responsibility for our choices because the law operates on the basis of coercion. Faith, as an orientation of the heart, opens one to the works of faith which emanate from the transformed inner person — the full reconciliation with the conscience. It restores to us the existential responsibility for our choices, including the choice to seek the help of divine grace for our transformation and perfecting.

If we view the Scripture as a whole, united revelation, then we understand this very well and we are able to understand what kind of faith and what kind of works are necessary for salvation.

Saving faith begins in the heart of one who desires righteousness, who begins voluntarily to strive toward good, and who feels the weight of evil. Such a person can recognize in the Person of Christ, perfect righteousness and deliverance from the Evil-One. This is the beginning. Accepting the fact that Christ is the Son of God who came to earth to save sinners is the beginning of faith — but it is not yet saving faith, because it is no more than the demons do, as Apostle

James says. We could make numerous comparisons, but suffice it to say that the Divine Scripture does not teach that one is saved by a mere conviction of the truth of Christ and the gospel. There is no faith without the struggle for moral perfection. Saving faith is in itself a moral struggle which begins, is maintained and becomes perfect by God's grace cooperating with man's work of directing his will to the good, towards selfless love by means of sobriety, fasting and prayer. To have faith means to be fully penetrated by Christ's life, and it is impossible to have saving faith without the works taught us by the Holy Apostle. These works are not at all the "works of law," which have already been fulfilled in Christ, but the struggle for liberation from the Evil- One, the struggle for moral perfection proclaimed in the Scripture, and taught by the apostles and the fathers.

Faith in Christ means renunciation of the world and a struggle for moral perfection and the acquisition of the Holy Spirit, as St Antony of Kiev expressed it:

> "...What characteristics identify that faith in Jesus Christ which, according to Apostle John, is sufficient for salvation .... Faith in Christ is saving faith when, proceeding from the demands of good conscience, it has respect not only for the Person of Jesus Christ, but to the entire inner content of that Person, to the qualities of life which He brought to earth in His Person."[33]

156

Faith is to accept Christ, not merely as a *way out* of any genuine labours, but to accept both Him and His commandments and teachings, and the example of His life on earth — to accept these, to believe that He will give us the grace to fulfil them, and to accept that He intended for us to fulfil all that He commanded.

Christ makes it abundantly clear that neither He nor His Kingdom is of this world, that friendship with the world is enmity with God. The ideal which Christ placed upon all who would have faith in Him is to be perfect as the Father is perfect. He bound this ideal and faith inseparably with renunciation of the world, of all worldly values and of the pleasure of the fallen flesh. The struggle to attain freedom from the Evil-One and to fulfil this ideal and all that goes with it comprises the spiritual life of the Orthodox Christian. The practical fulfilment of what we have said here is possible for every Orthodox person, and the means of its fulfilment is clearly evident in the nature and life of the Holy Church which is one, visible and undivided.

We have set forth four basic aspects of the goals of Orthodox Christian asceticism or spiritual struggle: the struggle to attain to selfless love; the struggle for freedom from the bonds of the Evil- One; the ascent in moral perfection towards a real, experiential knowledge of God; and becoming perfect as God is perfect. This struggle constitutes saving faith as it is taught in the Divine Scripture, which the Holy Church has given us. We have mentioned also the necessity to renounce this world of passions and to transfer all our

157

allegiance, hopes and concerns to the heavenly kingdom, to the world to come. These are all goals and ideals clearly demonstrated in the life of Christ on earth and saliently set forth in His own words. The life of Christ demonstrates precisely this transfer of aspirations and allegiance from this passionate, sinful world to that peaceful, sacred world, from this principality of evil to that Kingdom of good, for which reason our holy and Godbearing father John Chrysostom calls out to us:

> *Why do you tarry there beyond the boundaries? Rise up, come forth and reclaim your ancient fatherland lost by Adam!*[34]

5
THE EXISTENTIAL NATURE OF REDEMPTION

Redemption is an ontological process, not an historical execution understood as a juridical payment to an all too human "god."

The Orthodox concept of redemption may be briefly epitomized as follows: while "atonement" is not an Orthodox Christian term or expression, we may look at its actual meaning. "Atonement" is really "to remove (or overcome) the cause of separation." In

158

other words, man is separated from God, which is the actual meaning of the word "sin" (that is, by his constant "missing of the mark"), and so he is in bondage to death (because he is separated from the only Source of life, not because God punishes man with death). Since man sins continually because of the power of death, sin separates man from God and death perpetuates the separation (and vice versa). By death, we fall short (again, by "missing the mark" — sin) of our original destiny, which is to live through unity with the Creator.

The following summary of the Orthodox teaching about redemption is drawn from works by Fr John Romanides:

Christ saves men, who have fallen through their own fault into the power of the devil, by breaking that power. He became Man for this purpose; He lived and died and rose again that He might break the chains by which men were bound. It is not His death alone, but the entire Incarnation, of which His death was a necessary part, that freed men from their captivity to Satan. By becoming Man, living a sinless life, and rising from the dead (which He could not have done unless He had first died), He introduced a new power into human nature. This power is bestowed on all men who are willing to receive it, through the Holy Spirit. Those who receive it are united with Christ in His Mystical Body, the Church; the corrupted human nature (the bad habits and evil desires, which St Paul calls "the old man": Rm.6:6; Eph.4: 22; Col.3:9) is driven out by degrees, until at last it is expelled altogether, and the redeemed person becomes entirely obedient to the will of God, as our Lord Himself was when on earth. The prisoner is set free from the inside; his mind and body are both chan ge d; he comes to know what freedom is, to desire it and, by the Holy Spirit working within him, to break his chains, turn the key and leave the dungeon. Thus, he is freed from the power of sin. God forgives him, as an act of pure love; but the condition of his forgiveness is that he must sin no more. "While we were yet sinners Christ died for us" (Rm.5:8-9) but, if we continue to be sinners, Christ's death for us will have been in vain; and we are made capable of ceasing to be sinners by the power of Christ's Resurrection, which has given us the power to struggle against sinfulness, toward moral perfection.

The advantage of this Orthodox teaching is that it is firmly based on the New Testament. "God was in Christ reconciling the world to Himself" (2Cor.5:19); the act of reconciliation is effected by God in the Person of His Son, for it is man that needs to be reconciled to God, not God that needs to be reconciled to man. Throughout the New Testament we find the proclamation that Christ has broken the power of the devil, to which mankind was subject (see Lk.10: 17-18); 11:22; 1Cor.15: 25; Gal.1:4; Col.2:15; 2Tm.1: 10; Hb.2:14; Jn.10:11; 12:31; 16:11; 1Jn.3:8; and frequently in Rev.). Moreover, this teaching of the atonement requires no "legal fiction" and attributes no immoral or unrighteous action to God. Man is not made suddenly good or treated as good when he is not good [the classical Protestant delusion]; he is forgiven not because he deserves to be forgiven, but because God loves him, and he is made fit for union with God by God's own power, his own will co-operating. He is saved from the power of sin by the risen life of Christ within him, and from the guilt of sin by God's forgiveness, of which his own repentance is a condition.

Thus, salvation consists in the union of the faithful with the life of God in the Body of Christ (the Holy Church) where the Evil-One is being progressively and really destroyed in the life of co-suffering love. This union is effected by Baptism (the Grace of regeneration) and fulfilled in the Holy Communion of the Body and Blood of Christ, and in the mutual, cooperative struggle of Orthodox Christians against the power and influence of the Evil-One. This is precisely why the last words of the "Lord's Prayer" are, "deliver us from the Evil-One," and *not* "deliver us from evil."

In order to emphasize the existential nature of salvation yet further, let us look at the twenty-fifty chapter of Matthew's Gospel:[35]

MATTHEW CHAPTER 25
The Great Moral Imperative Restated:
Virtue without humanity is of no value;
there is no salvation without love of neighbours.

Then shall the kingdom of heaven be likened to ten virgins who took their lamps and went forth to meet the bridegroom. Five of them were wise, and five were foolish.

Those who were foolish took their lamps but did not take any oil with them: But the wise took oil in their vessels with their lamps.

While the bridegroom tarried, they all slumbered and slept. At midnight there was a cry made, `Behold, the bridegroom cometh; go out to meet him.' Then all those virgins arose, and trimmed their lamps. And the foolish said unto the wise, `Give us of your oil; for our lamps have gone out.' But the wise answered, saying, `We cannot, lest there not be enough for us and you: but go to those who sell, and buy [some] for yourselves.' And while they went to buy, the bridegroom came; and those who were ready went in with him to the marriage: and the door was shut. Afterward the other virgins came, saying, `Lord, Lord, open to us.' But He answered and said, `I tell you in truth, I do not know you.' (1-12)

We hear once more the enigmatic parable of the ten virgins. Such a story provides fuel for many and varied sermons. One can weave any number of moral and spiritual meanings, injunctions or encouragement from it, however, let us stay close to the interpretations of the Holy Fathers.

St Mark of Ephesus, informs us that the "virgins"

162

are a reference to the human souls. When the Lord says, "they slumbered and slept," He means that the persons had died and their souls, not able to receive the fulness of their reward, tarried at the very gates of Paradise awaiting the coming of Christ and the general resurrection.[36]

Chrysostom takes us further "The `lamps' he says, "signify the gift of virginity...by `oil', [He indicates] humanity — almsgiving, help [given] to those who are in need."[37]

All ten virgins had the same level of "correct behaviour," they had fulfilled the requirements of a moral code. Thinking that such legal morality was sufficient to open the gates of Paradise for them, they neglected the greater part of a moral life. Morality consists far more in how well we care for one another than it does in what kind of behaviour we demand of others.

The oil which the five foolish virgins had not acquired was that very humanity, the greater part of morality: that is, to cherish and nourish one's neighbours, the care of the poor, the dispossessed, the disenfranchised, the weak and all those in need. The Great Moral Imperative of Christ, to love the Lord our God, and our neighbours as ourselves, and the injunction to do to others what we would have them do to us. If all "the law and the prophets" hang on the first and greatest of these imperatives — love of God and neighbour — then all other acts and concepts of morality must have these as their focus and centre.

163

Every true concept of the moral life must flow from the great moral imperative. No matter how correct our behaviour, nor how clear our faith, the door of Paradise will not be open to us if we have only the lamps of correctness but have neglected the oil of humanity.

Matthew 25:13-30

Watch therefore, for ye know neither the day nor the hour wherein the Son of man cometh.

For the kingdom of heaven is as a man travelling into a far country, who called his own servants, and delivered unto them his goods. And unto one he gave five talants, to another two, and to another one; to every man according to his several ability; and straightaway took his journey. Then he that had received the five talants went and traded with the same, and made them other five talants. And likewise he that had received two, he also gained other two. But he that had received one went and digged in the earth, and hid his lord's money. After a long time the lord of those servants cometh, and reckoneth with them. And so he that had received five talants came and brought other five talants, saying, Lord, thou deliveredst unto me five talants: behold, I have gained beside them five talants more. His lord said unto him, Well done, thou good and faithful servant: thou hast been faithful over a few things, I will make thee ruler over many things: enter thou into the joy of thy lord. He also that had received two talants came and said, Lord, thou deliveredst unto me two talants: behold, I have gained two other talants beside them. His lord said unto him, Well done, good and faithful servant; thou hast been faithful over a few things, I will make thee ruler over many things: enter thou into the joy of thy lord.

Then he which had received the one talant came and said, Lord, I knew thee that thou art an hard man, reaping where thou hast not sown, and gathering where thou hast not strowed:

And I was afraid, and went and hid thy talant in the earth: lo, there thou hast that is thine.

His lord answered and said unto him, Thou wicked and slothful servant, thou knewest that I reap where I sowed not, and gather where I have not strowed:

Thou oughtest therefore to have put my money to the exchangers, and then at my coming I should have received mine own with usury.

Take therefore the talant from him, and give it unto him which hath ten talants. For unto every one that hath shall be given, and he shall have abundance: but from him that hath not shall be taken away even that which he hath. And cast ye the unprofitable servant into outer darkness: there shall be weeping and gnashing of teeth.

The parable of the silver talants follows immediately upon the story of the ten virgins. First, Christ shows us that the care of others is a necessary element of true morality. Indeed *all* moral behaviour must flow from the heart, motivated by love in order to have value for our salvation.

Now He speaks of a certain treasure which the Master had entrusted to His servants. Though spoken in earthly concepts, we are called to understand them in a spiritual manner. What is the great treasure which the Saviour has bestowed upon all who open themselves to faith? Is it not the unselfish love, even of co-suffering love bestowed by the One Who "so loved the world that He gave His only begotten Son..." and the One Who laid down His life even for the wicked, for us "while we were yet sinners?"

To one servant, he gave five silver talants, to another two, to the third, one. To each according to the individual strength of each, he gave justly, not wishing to overburden any. Did not all believe — for all were His servants; did not all have faith? Surely, for they all received the gifts given to the faithful. Did they not understand that the gifts of grace, the gift of a saving love, was one that they should invest in humanity and make gains for the Gospel, for the heavenly kingdom? They understood, for all demonstrated by their actions that they were responsible for both the treasure and the trust that had been given to them.

When we read that all were servants and all were entrusted with a heavenly treasure, we are informed that all obeyed a law and equally fulfilled a code of behaviour. One, however like the foolish virgins, allowed the gift to die within him. He fulfilled the legal norm — he did not steal the master's silver. He was moral, for he preserved what was entrusted to him without using it for his own ends, but returned it to its rightful owner. Why was this not sufficient?

Let us learn the meaning of this parable from the River Jordan and its two seas. The Jordan carries fresh water into the Sea of Galilee, and this lake is full of life. For thousands of years, fishermen have harvested a living from it. That same Jordan carries fresh water from Galilee into the Dead Sea. The Dead Sea is well named, because it has no fish and sustains no life. Why are the two seas of the River Jordan so different? Because the fresh water that flows into the Sea of Galilee flows out again on the other side. It nourishes a long valley before ending in the Dead Sea. Water does not flow out of the Dead Sea. It stagnates and evaporates. The water is no longer fresh and it does not support fish.

In order for it to remain life-bearing, the gifts of God's love must flow out of us toward others, while remaining intact within us. If we rather "bury it in the ground" until the master's return, it stagnates and does not support spiritual life.

The investment of silver talants which Christ has given us is the ability to carry on His ministry of co-suffering love and spiritual healing in the world. Together with the gifts of grace and love, we are given the ability to fulfil the great moral imperative: to actually cherish and nourish our neighbour as ourselves, while ascending in love toward God, so that we can truly receive the gift of loving Him with our whole mind, body and soul.

Here again, we learn that morality consists far more in how well we care for one another than in what sort of behaviour we demand of others. Belief and correct behaviour without humanity will not open the gates of Paradise to us.

Here he says that the master took a long journey, and after a long time he returned. In the first parable, He says that the bridegroom tarried in coming, but in both, it is clear that the lord appeared at a time unexpected. By this, He warns that you cannot live according to the spirit of darkness saying, "I will live without regard to God or man until just before He comes, and then I will repent and live according to His commandments just before that day. In this way, I will enter Paradise." Wherefore He says, "Watch, for you do not know the day or hour when the Son of Man comes."

Lest we fail to understand the inner meaning of these two parables, our Saviour adds an epilogue more stern and pointed. He summarizes the parables with an clear explanation of their inner meaning, a restatement in bold of the Great Moral Imperative:

> *When the Son of man shall come in his glory, and all the holy angels with him, then shall he sit upon the throne of his glory: And before him shall be gathered all nations: and he shall separate them one from another, as a shepherd divideth his sheep from the*

goats: And he shall set the sheep on his right hand, but the goats on the left.

Then shall the King say unto them on his right hand, Come, ye blessed of my Father, inherit the kingdom prepared for you from the foundation of the world: For I was hungry, and ye gave me food: I was thirsty, and ye gave me drink: I was a stranger, and ye took me in: Naked, and ye clothed me: I was sick, and ye visited me: I was in prison, and ye came unto me.

Then shall the righteous answer him, saying, Lord, when did we see thee hungry, and fed thee? or thirsty, and gave thee drink? When did we see thee a stranger, and took thee in? or naked, and clothed thee? Or when did we see thee sick, or in prison, and came unto thee?

And the King shall answer and say unto them, Verily I say unto you, Inasmuch as ye have done it unto one of the least of these my brethren, ye have done it unto me.

Then shall he say also unto them on the left hand, Depart from me, ye cursed, into everlasting fire, prepared for the devil and his angels: For I was hungry, and ye gave me no food: I was thirsty, and ye gave me no drink: I was a stranger, and ye took me not in: naked, and ye clothed me not: sick, and in prison, and ye visited me not.

Then shall they also answer him, saying, Lord, when did we see thee hungry, or athirst, or a stranger, or naked, or sick, or in prison, and did not minister unto thee?

Then shall he answer them, saying, Verily I say unto you, Inasmuch as ye did it not to one of the least of these, ye did it not to me.

And these shall go away into everlasting punishment: but the righteous into life everlasting.

Does our Saviour discount the struggle to lead a moral life, that is, to conduct ourselves in an appropriate manner according to Scripture? Not at all, for the very fact that only those who possessed the lamps were seen waiting at the gate of Paradise, and only those who, by faith had become His servants received the talants. He wishes us to understand, however, that correct behaviour cannot be a substitute for the great Moral Imperatives of love; moreover a professed love of God is of no value without a very real love of neighbour, and without regard to His teachings. To this end, the beloved Apostles tells us that,

If a man say, 'I love God,' and hateth his brother, he is a liar: for he that loveth not his brother whom he hath seen, how can he love God whom he hath not seen?

And this commandment have we from him, That he who loveth God loveth his brother also. Whosoever believeth that Jesus is the Christ is born of God: and every one that loveth him that begat loveth him also that is begotten of him. By this we know that we love the children of God, when we love God, and keep his commandments. For this is the love of God, that we keep his commandments: and his commandments are not grievous. (1 John 4:20-5:3)

How, then, shall we understand the separation of the sheep from the goats on the Great and Holy Day, in the context of all that has been said above? Our holy and God- bearing father Isaak of Nineveh, in the grace of the Holy Spirit, says:

I also maintain that those who are punished in Gehenna are scourged by the scourge of love. Nay, what is so bitter and vehement as the torment of love? I mean those who have become conscious that they have sinned against love suffer greater torment thereby than by any fearsome punishment which can be conceived. For the sorrow caused in the heart by sin against love is more piercing than any torment. It would be improper for a man to think that sinners in Gehenna are deprived of the love of God. Love is the offspring of knowledge of the truth which, as is commonly confessed, is given to all. The power of love works in two ways: it torments sinners, even as happens here when a friend suffers from a friend; but it becomes a source of joy for those who have observed its duties. According to my understanding this is the torment of Gehenna: bitter regret. But love inebriates the souls of the sons of heaven by its delectability.

"…. following a saying of the Apostle, `A conscience un-condemned is a witness of itself'… [cp.

171

Rm.2:15]. *(Homily 84.)*

ENDNOTES:

[1]. The *Didascalion* is a very ancient text written by the disciples of the Apostles as a collection of what they were taught by them.. St Ignatios (+107) wrote 7 leters, addressed to Churches in Asia Minor. Since he is known to have been consecrated by Apostle John, his letters have great authority in the Orthodox Church.

[2]. This article appeared in an older edition of the Greek Orthodox Theological Review. In fact, I read it in the vestibule of a Greek church where I was sitting because, at the time, the Greek chanting was rather tiresome to me (but then, I was only in my mid-teens at the time).

[3]. This is not the place or the level at which we should discuss "apophatic" theology. Let us simply note that "apophatic theology" is a realisation that our ability to know is limited, and that God is so different from us that we cannot offer any true definitions, sets of facts or descriptions of God that would actually be true. Allow me to suggest that, for our purposes here, "apophatic" means an informed unknowingness.

[4]. Theoria is a word borrowed from the Greek philosophers. Essentially, it means "contemplation." However, in our usage of the word, it includes "vision" and "revelation."

[5]. The confusion about the terms righteous and just and righteousness and juridical justification are a prime example. St James the Apostle was known as "James the Righteous," because of his diligent fulfilment of Jewish law and tradition. Now, we often see him referred to as "James the Just," with no explanation of why he is called "just." Metropolitan Antony Khrapovitsky, in his Moral Idea of the Dogma of Redemption, say: "In the New Testament, and particularly with St Paul, the concept of justification does not at all have such a juridically specific significance, but it really signifies righteousness, i.e., blamelessness, passionlessness and virtue, which concept is expressed by the Greek word δικαιοσύνη which is synonymous with αγιωσύνη; αρετή, etc. This was corroborated by the talented and highly erudite Professor Kliuchevsky (a historian rather than a theologian) who stated that he studied many ancient Greek juridical transcripts and documents and he could state that the concept δικαιοσύνη has, in every case, a moral significance and never a juridical sense, which is expressed in Greek by the word δίκη.

The conversation among the four of us about the terms "righteousness" and "justification," that is, about the ethical (moral) and

172

juridical understandings of redemption, took our opponent (M. D. Muretov) by surprise. Subsequently I observed that there were, on our side, incomparably stronger arguments than the simple interpretation of texts within the context of this conversation. The fact is that even in the Russian version of the Bible, which bears the marks of Protestant influence (which can be observed in almost all the words set in italics in the New Testament, i.e., the conjectures of the translators, and in the preference of the late Hebrew canon of the Old Testament, to the correct, Septuagint), the word, "justification" is forced into Apostle Paul's mouth only seven times, while he uses "righteousness" sixty-one times. Moreover, of these seven instances, "justification" [Opravdanie] is introduced erroneously three times instead of "righteousness" [Pravednost] (.i.e., instead of *pravda* or *pravednost* as In the Slavonic, corresponding to the Greek *dikaioseni* (such an eror occurs in Rm.3:24; 2Cor.3:9; Gal.2:21) where the context requires a moral (ethical) concept, and not a juridical one. This is true also of the other words of Apostle Paul which, even in the Russian text are rendered as *pravda*.)
, as both the Greek and the Slavonic texts read. Not once does the Slavonic text render the word δικαιοσύνη as "justification," but always as "righteousness." The Slavonic translators rendered as "justification" only the Greek words δικαίωσις and δικαίομα terms whose concepts are the opposite of condemnation or accusation, and which were used by the apostle in precisely this context, in contrast to these (i.e., condemnation or accusation) (for example in Rm.4:25; 5:16, 18; 8:4). To top it off, even the Slavonic translators erroneously render the Greek terms δικαίωσις and δικαίομα as "[juridical] justification" where these terms actually signify "law," "regulation" (for example, Rm.1:32; 2:26; Hb.9:1,10; also Lk.1:6; Rev.15:4). From all this, it is quite evident that the Pauline term δικαιοσύνη ("righteousness") received its juridical character among our scholastic theologians, not from Divine Scripture, but from Lutheran theology. Moreover, .Dr Alexandre Kalomiros points out that in Scripture, *dikaioseni*, is used to render the Hebrew word *tsedaka*, which means precisely, "the divine energy which accomplishes man's salvation," and indicates "restoration" rather than "atonement." Moreover it is closely synonymous with the Hebrew words *hesed* (mercy; compassion; love) and *emeth* (fidelity; truth).

[6]. The Holy Fathers developed a theology by expanding on the elements found in the Symbol in the process of expressing them more clearly and defending them against critics.

[7]. Rahner, Karl. *Theological Dictionary*, Herder, Freiberg, 1961. See Khrapovitsky, Saint Antony, "Moral Idea of the Dogma of Redemption," in *The Moral Idea of the Main Dogmas of the Faith*, Synaxis Press, 1984.

[8]. Retributive justice is actually not justice at all, rather it is revenge. Retributive justice, like Substitutionery Sacrifice, make forgiveness impossible. Forgiveness and punishment are mutually exclusive concepts. It is possible to have one or the other, but never both.

[9]. "Highlights in the debate over Theodore of Mopsuestia's Christology...", *Greek Orthodox Theological Review*, vol.5, no.2, 1959-60. Fn. 153, p.183.

[10]. From the time of Augustine of Hippo, Western theology began to develop on a basis of adaptations of Platonic thought and predispositions to basic Christian teachings. In the era of the scholastics, Aristotelianism replaced Platonism as the basis of Western theology — both Latin and Protestant. The variety of this Aristotelianism, however, was peculiar in its earlier years, in that it was taken from the interpretations of Aristotle made by the Moslem philosopher Avicenna. Indeed, the *Summa Theologica* of Aquinas is very heavily indebted to the Moslem sage's thought. See Papademetriou, G., *Introduction to Saint Gregory Palamas*, Philosophical Library, N.Y. 1973; Meyendorff, J., *A Study of Gregory Palamas*, The Faith Press, London, 1964; Romanides, Rev. J., "Notes on the Palamite Controversy," Greek Orthodox Theological Review, vol.6, no.2, 1960-61, pp.186-205; Afnan, S., *Avicenna, His Life and Works*; Allen & Unwin, London.

[11]. This *humanism* has nothing to do with humanitarianism. Modern humanism is predicated on Protagoras' idea that man is the measure of all things, and this, as a utilitarian philosophy of the industrial revolution, is the real source of man's destruction of the environment (the idea that any authentic Christian understanding of man's mastery over the earth was responsible for the modern ecological crises is simply fraudulent).

[12]. The Divine Liturgy was written by Apostle James, evidently within a year of the Ascension of Christ. Apostle Mark and others of the Apostles also gave directions for the celebration of the Divine Liturgy, as they had learned from Christ. Sts Basil the Great and John Chrysostom combined all the Apostolic Liturgies into one, so that there would be complete liturgical harmony throughout the Church.

[13]. This is why one encounters so much Gnostic ecstaticism, mysticism and occultism in the history of Western monasticism and Protestant spirituality. The philosophical dryness and remoteness of theology in the West left spiritual endeavour without vital formation and guidance.

[14]. Conversation with Motovilov (also published under the title "Wonderful Revelation to the World." (Holy Trinity Monastery, Jordanville, N.Y., 1965)

[15]. Philosopher of Education Moses Hadas makes the perfectly correct observation that: "What the moralist's suspicion of material progress is based upon, ultimately, is the inveterate notion that body and soul are more less disparate entities, so that attention to one must imply neglect of the other. The origin of this dualism of body and soul, at least in the western tradition, is the teachings of the Orphic [Gnostics]...." *Old Wine, New Bottles* (Giant Cardinal Editions, N.Y., 1963) p.4

This is true, but perhaps one should observe that both the dualism and the fantasies about a pre-mechanistic golden age, which still haunts our own scholastic fundamentalists, derives from Socrates and Plato, who considered mechanistic physics degrading. The dualism originated with Orphic Gnosticism, but the Dialogues of Plato are the primary transmitters of the idea to the West.

[16]. The Greek words "mystical," "mystery," "mystagogia," etc. have nothing to do with *mysticism*, despite the similarity in the sound of the words. In Orthodox theology, as in proper Greek, the words "mystical," etc, simply indicate that things have a deeper meaning than appears on the surface. A "holy mystery" refers to the mystery of the work of divine grace, which obviously is not readily comprehensible by human reasoning, etc.

[17]. The Gnostic heresies often had a concept of a special "ascetic theology," which was somehow separate from "regular theology." This is also reflected in the Latin division between mysticism and theology, and it was also reflected in the Gnostic thought of the late Fr Seraphim Rose in the Orthodox Church. Because of it, Fr Rose introduced, or sought to introduce, a number of Gnostic heresies into the Russian Orthodox Church, where they seem to have been relatively welcome. Fr Seraphim Rose's heresies tend to be Manichean and Platonistic in character, and they took advantage of the Bogomil residue which is found in Russian and other Slavic folk superstitions and popular religious tales. Among his heresies are the dogmatization of the aerial toll house myth (a direct import from Manichean and Mandean Gnosticism), Platonistic dualism, condemned already by the fathers of the Church, the notion of wandering souls and free acting disembodied spirits, the gnostic heresy of "subtle bodies," and the notion that souls can be in hell before the second coming, and without their bodies (a teaching condemned by the Orthodox delegation at the Council of Florence, particularly in the works of St Mark of Ephesus).

[18]. See Khrapovitsky, Saint Antony, *The Moral Aspect of the Main Dogmas of the Church*, Synaxis Press, 1984.

[19]. Lossky, V., *The Mystical Theology of the Eastern Church*, James Clark & Co., London, 1968.

175

[20]. "Mystical" is not to be construed as having to do with mysticism. "Mystical" indicates "hidden" and relates to things which are beyond our comprehension until we are aided by God's grace in experiencing things which we cannot comprehend by the processes of human reasoning.

[21]. i.e., an "ontological process."

[22]. Which is why, in the Orthodox Church, there is no such thing as "canonization of saints," but rather, saints are said to be "glorified." Glorification is the end toward which we struggle, and this depends upon the complete acquisition of the Holy Spirit.

[23]. *Against Eunomius*, Discourse 3.

[24]. It should be noted that mysticism almost always perceives a contradiction or even an enmity between body and soul, material and immaterial.

[25]. A person's moral failings, vices and problems cannot be healed by legislation, contempt, condescension or punishment, nor by the fear of such things, but only by the effective, grace-filled power of a co-suffering love. Let us recall that the woman taken in adultery (Jn.8:4) knew very well that the penalty was being publicly stoned to death. Neither this punishment nor the fear of this punishment was sufficient to deter her from her falling. Indeed, Christ debased and shamed those who thought it would, or who thought that morality was a condition that could be legislated. When he refused to condemn her, but lovingly told her: "neither do I accuse you, but go, and sin no more," what power or strength did He impart to her so that she would be able to obey this loving injunction? It was the power of His own co-suffering love that healed her and delivered her. Indeed, the ideal of co-suffering love is the basis of Orthodox Christian dogmatics and its moral concept. Let us say that it is the basis of all our theology. Let us also make it clear that morality cannot be legislated, nor can it be enforced by law; for, no deed has any moral value whatsoever unless it proceeds from the heart, motivated by unselfish love.

The sins of each and all are our own sins, for if we do not actually commit them, we nevertheless are both capable and inclined to do so. Thus, when one judges and condemns one's brother or sister, one is actually condemning himself. The power of serving for the regeneration of a fellow human being is found not in the practice of theoretical morals, but in the miracle of co-suffering love. This is the mystery of the Cross. The morality of Juridical Justification theology is pagan and unworthy of the Gospel of Christ.

[26]. It must be noted that the term translated as "kingdom" in the English version of the Scripture does not signify a created kingdom with some "geographical location," ruled by God, but signifies the uncreated rule and reign of God. This is why the Church is precisely the kingdom of God manifested on earth: because it is in the Church, separated from the spirit and principality of this world that this uncreated reign of God is manifested. See, for example, Rev. Dr. John Romanides, *Church Synods and Civilisation*, **THEOLOGIA**, Vol.63, Issue 3, July-September, 1992.

[27]. 1Cor.13:12f

[28]. One is tempted to say "knowledge *of* God" (theognosis). Technically this is not correct, but the idea is to know God through an experiential relationship with Him, guarded by the expressed theology from delusion, pantheism and error. In Orthodox Christianity, theology is not divorced from experience.

[29]. "The Life of the Prophet Moses," *Works*.

[30]. Apostle Paul tells us that we are reconciled by Christ's death, and saved by His life (Rm.5:10). Christ fulfilled all righteousness for us by ascending the Cross in wholly self-less love, and conquering in Himself all our passions and sickness, finally destroying the power of death, which separates us from God and keeps us in bondage to the Evil-one. Thus, His death, by which He fulfilled all righteousness (essentially, complete, unselfish, co-suffering love) reconciles us, and His rising again saves us from bondage to Satan through death by conquering its power.

[31]. *Pravoslavnoe Dogmaticheskoe Bogoslovie*, Holy Trinity Monastery, Jordanville, N.Y., 1963, pp.18-19.

[32]. For example, it may be *subjective:* a personal conviction and commitment—that I believe or *objective:* as in "The Faith" — what I believe (e.g., the Trinity).

[33]. Khrapovitsky, Metropolitan Antony, "What is Saving Faith?" in *Collected Essays*, Synaxis Press (to be published).

[34]. Homily on the Gospel of John, *Works*.

[35]. This homily is taken from *HOMILIES OF MATTHEW'S GOSPEL*, Lazar Puhalo, (Synaxis Press, 1998).

[36]. St Mark of Ephesus, *Ten Arguments Against Purgatory*.

[37]. Homily 78 on Matthew's Gospel.

VII
THE EXISTENTIAL NATURE
OF ORTHODOX CHRISTIAN
SYSTEMATIC PRAYER

An extemporaneous talk given at the
St Gregory Palamas Conference
San Luis Obispo, California., 1999
Transcribed from audio tape by Anastasia Birou and
and edited for publication by Makary Bieloivanov.

1
THE PROPHETIC MINISTRY

Before I speak about prayer, there are a few observations I would like to add to the previous paper on *The Appearance of the Holy Man*[1]. When we talk about the appearance of the "holy man" as an historical phenomenon, we are speaking also of certain major changes in society, and in the life of the Church. There are certain movements and changes in the structure of society, and in the way life in the Church is being shaped, which appear to necessitate a passage from the need for the ministry of kerygma to the ministry of prophecy. There is a time when we need prophets instead of preachers. Prophets do not teach in the same way that preachers do, even if the preachers are truly Orthodox. These holy men are usually hesychasts who have been formed in the traditional systematic prayer of Orthodoxy.

At the present time, within the Orthodox Church,

the crisis of Ecumenism is substantially undermining the Orthodox Christian Gospel and leading Orthodox Christians into the spirit of reductionism and minimalism common to Liberal Protestantism.

The hesychasts or holy men and women of any particular historical era are people with a prophetic ministry, a prophetic gift, who have seen the generation of corruption within the Church, a stepping away from an effective prayer life, and an abandonment of the Orthodox Christian system of prayer which we have by revelation. To say that they see some *unique* corruption in society would be rather utopian. There is always a corruption in society at large, as there was in Israel, in the Christian Roman Empire, including the Byzantine period of that empire. The prophetic ministry in Israel did not concern the world at large, but was concerned with the life of that nation which constituted, at that time, the Church of the living God. The prophetic ministry manifested by the appearance of the "holy men" in the life of the Orthodox Church has not concerned the life of the world at large, but rather has concerned that which impacts directly on the lives of the faithful within the Church. St Symeon the New Theologian was not overly concerned about the civil society around him, but focused his prophetic ministry on the life of the Church, the monastic communities and hierarchs in particular. There is little use in criticizing civil society while the leaders in the Church are incapacitating the Church's ability to minister to the world. Ultimately, the witness of St Gregory Palamas was just as effective after the Turkish conquest as it had been before it. The leaders of civil society, the Paleologoi, Kantecuzene and the Serbian Tsar Stevan Dushan, in their overweening greed and lust for power, incapacitated what was left of the state and rendered it incapable of surviving the Turkish invasion, but the witness of St Gregory Palamas and the hesychasts strengthened the inner life of the Church, the inner life of prayer of the faithful, and remained a force after the secular state, that pitiful remnant of the Eastern Roman or Byzantine Empire had ceased to exist. The rise of the holy man, usually from among the monastics, with a prophetic ministry, is a gift of grace to the Church. If it impacts at all on civil or secular society it is because this ministry has been heeded and re-enabled the Church to minister to the world in truth — not just the truth of words, but the truth of deeds and of the lives lived by the hierarchs and the people. This ministry is not manifested in histrionic sermons or angry moralistic preaching, but in the transformation of the lives of the faithful and the manifestation of such transformed, even transfigured, lives in the world. The core of this prophetic ministry, this prophetic teaching of these holy men and women, is prayer.

2
THE PROPHETIC MINISTRY
AND PRAYER

Be still and know that I am God (Ps.47:10)

There is a difference between having a system of prayer, prayer with a meaningful form, and a formalism in prayer just as there is a difference between formalism in worship and having a meaningful liturgical form of worship service — a form established by the Holy Spirit. The form of worship conveys the inner Gospel message of that worship and formal liturgical worship was established directly by God from the beginning of the human race. Televangelism represents formalism of preaching and worship, but is devoid of meaningful form and established only by the imagination and traditions of men. Formal liturgical worship is based in revelation and is filled with meaning and understanding. It has purpose, direction and destination, and is an antidote to spiritual chaos and confusion. The systematic prayer which has always been an instrument of the prophetic ministry within the Orthodox Church is likewise an antidote to chaos and confusion. Such prayer has not only a clear meaning, but it has a clearly defined purpose and destination.

When a person is called upon to say a prayer impromptu in front of an audience, or told to have a prayer ready next week for some event, they are concerned with what the people of the audience are going to think of them while they are saying this prayer that they have made up. Such prayer is genuinely formalistic and often egoistic. One is not just trying to address God; one is also trying to impress the audience even if only subconsciously. This is what formalism actually consists in. A form or system of prayer can become formalistic to an individual, no matter that it is revealed by the grace of the Holy Spirit, and the prophetic ministry actually tries to restore the perspective of such people.

Civil society in Byzantium had developed such a deadly formalism that the whole structure of government was crippled by the most inane, useless and mindless rituals and formality which even the Emperor himself was obliged to go through, instead of tending to the business of the Empire. This naturally spilled over into every class of society, especially the upper classes. The leaders of the Church had become corrupted by this degenerate spirit also, and this in turn crippled the preaching of the Gospel and darkened the path of salvation. At such a critical time in history the prophetic ministry was again manifested in the form of the hesychastic renewal: the prophetic ministry was directly tied to the *meaning and purpose* of prayer. It is recorded that on one occasion, one of the senators was sitting in his place in the senate in Constantinople, at a time of crisis and emergency for the state. The senator was very deep in hesychastic prayer. One of the other senators turned to the Emperor and suggested that they "call him back" out of his state of prayer so they could ask his advice. The Emperor replied, "Leave him alone. He is doing much more good for us there where he is than we are here where we are." Ultimately, any solution to the problems of the State would depend on solutions to the fundamental problems of the fallen human nature. Those solutions certainly cannot be found in the almost brutish and hypocritical hypermoralism[2] of televangelists and the twisted, deformed ideology of the Falwells and Dobsons of this world. They do not look for the actual causes of problems, rather, like Hitler, they oversimplify in order to gain support — primarily financial support, and instead of trying to help heal the people's problems, they seek to persecute them, to stir up hatred against them and advocate their own version of the "ultimate solution." The prophetic ministry seeks the solution to problems in the nature of the fallen human condition. The solution remains to be found in the struggle for transformation and the assimilation of the renewed nature in Jesus Christ. We attain this, only with great effort, by the acquisition of the Holy Spirit, and this requires a unique life of prayer and fasting. The preacher seeks to expound the elementary things of the Gospel — the sincere preacher, honourably, the hate monger and "for profit" preacher, dishonourably. The true prophet is not a soothsayer nor an entertaining predictor of the future. The prophet seeks to open the human nature to the light of grace, first to expose and then to heal. This is why I would identify the prophetic ministry with the holy man who preaches true prayer, a life of prayer and hesychastic prayer in particular. True prophets who have received some warning about the future which God commands them to proclaim, do so in order to arm people with spiritual struggle, prayer and repentance so that they will not be found wanting when those things do come to pass.

That is all I wanted to say about the holy man: he is a transference to the prophetic ministry. If we look at the Old Testament prophets, the prophets were always on the periphery of society, they were not at the heart of society. No prophet can be an integral part of the society around him and fulfil his prophetic ministry. The prophetic ministry automatically places a person on the periphery of society, as it did in the case of St Symeon the New Theologian. First of all, he has to stand back and look at society from its outer boundaries, and he cannot be in the midst of it and still do that. Secondly, a prophet can never be accepted by society, because he is peeling away the scab over the sores of the society, and because he is offering a critique of society in the light of divine grace, with the grace of the Holy Spirit that has been imparted to him by God. We have a certain form of prophet in literature, the arts and even cartoons. If you look carefully at the cartoons in the newspapers, you will see that there is a certain amount of social critique going on in them. There are different kinds of prophecy; there is a form of prophecy given by the careful and concerned social observer with no gifts other than his or her natural astuteness, and there are those prophets who are clearly inspired by the Holy Spirit. The latter has to somehow stand on the periphery of society and look in lovingly, with sorrow rather than with self-righteous condemnation. This is precisely what the holy man who arises at particular times in our history does. This is what the holy men at the end of the Byzantine Empire did. Foremost among them was Saint Gregory Palamas, the preacher of prayer, having received divine grace from the Holy Spirit. They had the gift of prophecy and they were making a critique of society in the light of that grace, not in order to condemn it, but in order to offer it healing, at least to those who had ears to hear the will of God. The primary vehicle for this healing was prayer — hesychastic prayer.

3
PRAYER WITH FOCUS AND PURPOSE

First, I want to discuss prayer with you, in particular, why we have both a system of prayer as well as the spontaneous prayer that we practise within the context of our own private lives, and formal prayers that are unified with the worshipping community within the liturgical context. When prayer is spoken about in our day, we often hear about it in an emotional way, most often with a theosophical and New Age spin. One hears the most astonishing assertions: if your television set is broken, put your hand on it and pray, and you might be able to heal it so you will not miss any of your favourite soap operas. People will tune in to a certain preacher on radio and they will place their hands on the radios in the theosophical seance type of holding hands which is popular among sectarians, and all pray to lose weight together. This is how inane and degenerate the concept of prayer has become. If there is no economic or material benefit to it, why bother to pray? We pray for material things, we pray that we will not have to suffer and endure anything in this life, even though Christ directly promised us that His true followers would have to endure much. For many, prayer life has turned into a form of egotism, a self-satisfaction, a self-endorsement, a plea for instant gratification. Ironically, even while religion hawkers are selling their own snake-oil systems of prayer, they are preaching against the systematic prayer of the Orthodox Christian Church. Televangelist prayer systems are designed with the promise that they will attract material well-being, health and happiness — the acquisition of some worldly state without the process of purification — while the systematic prayer of the Orthodox Church has a definite and clear-cut spiritual goal and destination. The reason people do not understand Orthodox Christian prayer is that their own prayer life seldom has any destination or concept of precisely what it is they are trying to accomplish in prayer. The necessity to struggle for the purification of the conscience (heart) does not even occur to them. Most people, when they pray, are not trying to accomplish anything except to satisfy some emotional need or perceived material need. Often, people pray because it is a

186

cultural exercise. In fact, even religion itself has become little more than a cultural affectation in our society. In America, many consider it a patriotic duty to be religious so they practise the cultural religion and pray because it is the proper thing to do. It is like singing "O Canada," "God Save the Queen," or "The Star-Spangled Banner." Even though religion and prayer may be a cultural affectation, they do not become an integral part of the soul of society. Religion and prayer fulfil a superficial emotional need in our lives, but we do not give it any depth, we do not give it any genuine meaning. Above all, we do not think of prayer in terms of the process of the purification of the conscience, the path toward illumination, and as an absolutely necessary part of the struggle for our salvation.

When our holy fathers and mothers examined the matter of prayer, they never even considered the idea that it was an "obligation" to God or that it was somehow done "for God's sake." We do not have to pray in order to inform God, to let Him know something He does not know. We pray in order to draw ourselves closer to God, because we really cannot know someone that we do not talk to; we cannot know someone that we refuse to have discourse with. So, we pray in order to bring ourselves closer to God and learn more about what He reveals to us about Himself. Many of the written prayers in the Church are designed to lead us into this kind of prayer. They instruct us and give us a ladder that we can climb in an ascent toward this knowledge and understanding of God, bringing us closer to Him. They also offer us a proper perspective on ourselves.

4
THE LORD'S PRAYER AS REVELATION
An Existentialist Understanding

The most formal of prayers is the "Lord's Prayer" itself. When we look at the Lord's Prayer, on the surface it appears very simple, but it is not simple at all. What is most astonishing about the Lord's Prayer is that in its profoundly simple beauty, such riches of theological knowledge are given.

The Lord's Prayer is actually quite complex. If we begin to think about the unknowable, unseen, incomprehensible, uncircumscribable God as our Father, it is an astonishing assertion. He is not like us at all. We have no genetic relationship to Him. He is absolutely unlike us in any way and yet we have to conceive of Him as our Father. Moreover, this has to deeply shape our emotional view of ourselves and our relationship with the universe. Yet we humans manage to trivialize that. In many modern Protestant hymnals and prayer books, we see such perversions as "our Father/ Mother Who is in heaven," "our Parents who are in Heaven," and perhaps even, "to whom it may concern," whatever phantasy people fall into these days. We trivialize our concept of God as Father and make it an empty, meaningless, emotional statement.

By trivializing the words and content of the Lord's Prayer, we trivialize both the meaning of God as our Father, the message of redemption and, indeed, Jesus Christ Himself. Do you see how easily we trivialize the words of Jesus Christ by rewriting the Lord's Prayer according to our own whims and fancies? Jesus Christ taught us to pray, "Our Father Who art in the Heavens—*o en tis ouranis.*" "In the Heavens," not "in Heaven," because God is everywhere present and fills all things. If we would take the time to contemplate the meaning of the words Jesus Christ has given us, perhaps it would be more difficult for us to trivialize them. The idea of God as our Father is astonishing. We must realize that God is our Father because he cared enough about us to adopt us as His children, to seek us and search us out to find those who were willing to become His children, in spite of our constant rebelliousness and self-will, and bring us into His own household and try to train us and bring us up in His way. It is an astonishing thing: "Our Father Who art in the Heavens." The word "heavens" refers to the material creation which we see when we look skyward — the moon, stars, planets, galaxies, and all that moves through the universe. The "heavens" has no mystical meaning, no metaphysical significance, it is just a bunch of material and energy that formed in the process of creation, but it does fill the universe and God does order and direct it. Our God is everywhere present and fills all things, and this is what Jesus Christ taught us when He instructed us to pray,

"Our Father Who art in the Heavens."[3] "Hallowed be Thy name, Thy rule and reign come, Thy will be done on earth as it is in heaven." The word that is used in the original Lord's Prayer does not signify simply "kingdom" in our earthly sense, rather it indicates the "rule and reign" of God. "Thy will be done on earth as it is in heaven." This time, our Lord Jesus Christ narrows the scope down. He taught us to pray "heaven," in the singular. He is no longer talking about the universe at large, but is using the word "heaven" in its abstract sense, the "kingdom of heaven," that unique place of God. The "kingdom of heaven" is not a geographical location, or a political or physical entity such as an earthly kingdom. The kingdom of heaven, God's Kingdom, is present and manifested wherever the rule and reign of God has been accepted. Great mysteries are being revealed to us in this prayer, and yet some jurisdictions of the Orthodox Church literally trivialize the words and teaching of Jesus Christ by self-willed rewording of this prayer, done primarily for the sake of Ecumenism.[4] The mystery of the fall of Satan from "heaven" is revealed in this prayer, for when we say, "on earth as it is in heaven," we acknowledge that the will of God has been *freely accepted* in that "place," if we may metaphorically call it a place. The rebellion of Satan against God was something permitted because God desires that each of His creatures should take a decision of their own free will, without compulsion, to be with Him or separate from Him. Love does not compel love, but desires that love be freely accepted and freely returned. Angels could not have been sentient, intelligent beings without freedom of will. Satan departed from heaven under the same circumstances that Adam and Eve departed from Paradise. A free will choice was made, and those angelic beings who chose to love God and remain united with Him, freely accepted His rule and reign, and were sealed in that choice forever. This is precisely what happens to those who depart this life in sincere faith. Thus, our Lord taught us to signify that unique "heaven" where the will of God is truly fulfilled, where the will of God rules and reigns in the minds and will of the angelic hosts. "Thy will be done on earth as it is in Heaven." The will of God is that all people should turn from their separation and live. The will of God is that all should freely accept His love and share in an everlasting life of blessedness. The will of God will be done on earth wherever the rule and reign of God has been freely accepted, which is why Jesus Christ told us that the kingdom of heaven is within us, even in our very hearts — that is, within those who, like the faithful angels, freely accept His rule and reign in their hearts. Thus, the way to bring about the rule and reign of God on earth, is to freely accept the rule and reign of God in our hearts. But the fulness of this message is also usually trivialized because so many people do not consider a correct translation of this prayer to be important, and they can think up a host of trivial excuses for not correcting their translations of it. It is also trivialized when one claims to "accept Jesus into his heart," but in fact, only so long as He doesn't bother us any, or make any noise down there or disturb us. We are not speaking here in terms of the novel concept of "accepting - Christ as your own personal Saviour" which was invented around the end of the 1800s by the Revivalists Movement. This concept is understood in a legalistic way. You accept Christ as your own personal Saviour and then He is obligated to save you, because now you have a legal agreement with Him. Such people forget that the old covenant was not a *legal agreement* between God and Israel; it was a *spousal relationship*. All the Holy Prophets, without exception, tried to remind Israel that they did not have a legal agreement with God but a spousal relationship with Him. A spousal relationship does not include non-involvement. Spouses do interject with each other and interject into each other's lives. Spouses have a relationship where they are quite free to be intimately involved in every aspect of each other's lives. The Church has a spousal relationship with God, and the will of God is done not where somebody just says, "Yes, I accept Jesus." The rule and reign is not simply a presence, it is a governance, it actually governs our lives and the structure of our being. Though we speak of the heart, of accepting Jesus into our hearts, we are talking about the conscience, which is the spiritual heart of man. The physical heart is an electro-mechanical pump. Our physical heart responds and reacts to emotional stimuli, but only because of hormones

192

released by the brain. It is neither the seat nor source of our emotions, disposition or faith. The spiritual heart of man is his conscience and the conscience is the ultimate judge of man. So the purification of the "heart," "accepting Jesus Christ into our hearts," involves allowing God to rule and reign in our *conscience*. We will talk about this in the context of prayer in a moment.

Our Father Who art in the Heavens, hallowed be Thy name, Thy kingdom come, Thy will be done on earth as it is in Heaven. Give us this day our daily superessential bread, "epiousion arton," "khleb nash nasushni." It doesn't say simply "daily bread," it says *"ton epiousion arton"* — the meaning is deeper than simply "daily" — our superessential bread, the bread of life. Give us today the bread of life, that superessential bread that comes down from the Father. Give us today participation in our Lord Jesus Christ, Who said, "I am the bread of life." The manna was not given by Moses. The manna, that life-saving bread in the desert, was given by God, and Jesus Christ is the *Bread of Life* that came down from the Father. Give us today participation in the "epiousion arton," the superessential bread of life, our Lord Jesus Christ.

"And forgive us our debts;" the word "trespasses" does not occur in the original. Forgive us this day our debts, *"ta ofelimata,"* as we forgive our debtors. There are two unforgivable sins mentioned in Scripture: blasphemy against the Holy Spirit and refusal to forgive. If you do not forgive, you will not be

193

forgiven. If you do not forgive, your Father Who is in Heaven will not forgive you. You close yourself off from forgiveness, by refusing to forgive if only because by refusing to forgive you deny or trivialize the meaning of Christ's ministry and refuse Him a place in your heart. When you refuse to forgive you reject the rule and reign of God in your life and your heart, and when the rule and reign of God is no longer there, the will of God is no longer done. The will of God is that we should forgive as He forgives.

"Forgive our debts as we forgive our debtors and lead us not into trials and tribulations, into temptation." Tempting or tempering is what a black-smith does when he wants to strengthen a steel object he has made. If you forge an axe blade, while it is red hot, you dip it under cold water to temper it. You tempt or temper the blade to make it harder and more durable. When we pray not to be delivered into temptation, we are not suggesting that God would deliver us into temptation in the way we usually think about it — the temptation to fall into separation from Him — but we are nevertheless, willing to accept it when God determines that we need to be exercised or tempered in order that we be strengthened.

"Lead us not into temptation, but deliver us from the evil one." Jesus Christ never said "deliver us from evil" and we trivialize both His word and Him when we allow the mis-translation to be used. Evil has no ontological existence, evil is not a thing, is not a being so we cannot be delivered from it as if it was our

194

captor. Evil is a condition of separation from the good. Deliver us from the Evil-One, [Sl. *ot lukavago*: Gr. *paniroui*]. Jesus Christ did not come down to earth to redeem us from God. He did not come down to satisfy God's need for justice, for God is not subject to immutable laws of the universe over which He has no power. Christ ransomed us from the power of the Evil-One, Satan, and our struggle, like that of the Hebrews in the Sinai Desert, is to keep from falling back into bondage. The phrase, "deliver us from the Evil-one" is a concise exposition of the meaning of redemption and a refutation of the Western doctrine of "the Atonement." Let us not trivialize Jesus Christ and His teaching, but rather let us accept His word and insist on praying the Lord's prayer as He taught it to us.

The idea that Christ came to take on our "just punishment" vicariously and deliver us from God's juridical justice and satisfy His offended majesty, is simply pagan. That is the concept which motivated pagans to sacrifice babies to Moloch and Baal. Our Lord Jesus Christ came to *redeem* us. You can only be redeemed from one to whom you are in bondage. We are not in bondage to God, we are in bondage to Satan through sin because sin separates us from God. We fall into bondage, we are "sold under sin" (Rm.7:14) by our own acts and deeds, by our own choice of actions, which cause us to fall short of the glory which God intended for us (Rm.3:23) and become separated from God and thus from life itself. We are redeemed

195

from the power of Satan and death, we are redeemed back to the household of God. This is revealed to us throughout the Old Testament in the laws of redemption. We see that revelation in the person who had the title of "first born," whether he was literally the "first born" of many children or an only child, or simply the one who held the position. In the concept of redemption and the Old Testament laws of redemption, the title "first born" is equivalent to "redeemer." The "first born" son of any household was obligated to redeem back to the father's house every seven years, any property, land, or real estate that had been alienated from the father's house. Every seven years he would redeem the alienated property for money if possible, but in any Jubilee year, he could redeem it without money, by demanding its return. Thus, the one who bore the position of "first born" bore the responsibility of redeemer. Our Lord Jesus Christ redeemed that which had been alienated from the Father's house, sold under sin, held in bondage to the fear of death by Satan. He redeemed us back to the Father's household. He did not redeem us *from* the Father, rather He "delivered us from the Evil-one."

The mystery of redemption is the mystery of the co-suffering love of God for mankind.

5
PRAYER AS PART OF
THE HEALING PROCESS

We have discussed all this because a deeper understanding of the prayer which Jesus Christ taught us, the "Lord's Prayer," will help us to form our perspective about what prayer actually means. Prayer is not a social affectation nor an emotional fulfilment, nor something that props up our ego, as it often happens. When we pray, we want to feel the presence of God in our lives and sense more deeply the presence of the grace of the Holy Spirit. This is a basic purpose of prayer. This, however, can be expressed at a shallow, emotional level where emotions can be mistaken for a real, prayerful relationship with Christ. Prayer has a great deal more to say to us and to give to us. Prayer is a part of the healing process. The ministry of Christ on earth was a healing ministry, not a jur-idical expedition. Christ came to heal the fallen human nature and restore it to unity with God, thus unity with life. All of us participate in one and the same human nature for there are not many human natures, but one and it is a fallen nature. Jesus Christ came to redeem our nature and restore the perfect human nature in Himself. By becoming participants in Jesus Christ, we become participants in the perfect human nature, which is fully united with God; we become partakers of the redeemed humanity, freed from the bondage of the fallen human nature. Despite the vain and, in some cases, blasphemous attempts to forge a rationalistic, juridical explanation based on the concepts of Roman and Germanic law, there would have been no other reason for God to become man. There would have been no need for God to become incarnate in the flesh. It would be useless had He not come to restore mankind to unity with Himself — or rather to facilitate and offer man the possibility of such unity. The whole life of Christ on earth is a revelation to us about the struggle for the reunion of man with God. It is made possible by Jesus Christ, but not made inevitable by Jesus Christ. It is up to us to accept and pursue this redemption, this healing and restoration.

The life of prayer has a great deal more to do with the healing process than we often consider. That is why we have a *system* of prayer. We are being systematically healed and prayer is a major part of that process. In addition to the systematic prayer which St Gregory Palamas and other holy fathers defended against the Augustinian West, we have those prayers that we pour out from our hearts in the fulness of our grief and joy "in our own closet" (Mt.6:6). When hesychastic prayer was being taught from the very earliest times, Apostle Paul's command to "pray without ceasing" (1Thes.5:17) was taken quite seriously. Systematic hesychastic prayer is the method revealed in the Church by which we may attain to ceaseless prayer and at the same time be protected from delusion in our prayer lives. It is a part of the healing process in much the same way that a prescription given by a physician is part of the healing process for infections and physical illnesses. That is why it includes something called guarding of the mind, both to prevent our falling into delusion and to help prevent a "reinfection" by whatever passions we are being healed of.

But prayer is very practical. It is not just an emotional or spiritual practice that leads us into some kind of mysticism or creates some form of "spirituality" for us. *Mysticism* and *mystical* do not equal the same thing. When we talk about mystical we are not talking about mysticism and when we talk about a spiritual life we are not talking about "spirituality," but I will explain why a little bit later.

We will understand the concept of prayer as part of the healing process if we look at the process by which sin daily enters our lives, and examine how prayer responds to that process. Let us look at how the holy fathers defined the entrance of sin into our lives, and the process by which it takes possession of our minds and often becomes an addiction that consumes our being. We will see how we use prayer to repel or heal ourselves from that invasion of the spiritual virus that is sin. Sin does not mean breaking the law; sin means to fall short of the mark or goal which God has set for us. The mark and goal of having good health is intervened by microbes, viruses, bacteria, and that sort of thing. The same is true of spiritual health. Sin is a spiritual microbe that invades the body and dwells parasitically within the body. It lurks parasitically in the flesh. We are concerned, therefore, with spiritual antibiotics. We are concerned with spiritually struggling against these microbes, these viruses of sin, deceit and delusion that take root in our being and become parasitically imbedded in us. They consume us not only as individual human beings but as societies, cultures and nations. The holy fathers and mothers of the desert knew very well exactly what they were talking about when they defined the process by which sin takes possession of us. They did not simply say "The devil made me do it." The devil may delude us or take advantage of what we have become willing to do or in bondage to, but if we know the process by which this take place, we are able to use prayer as a powerful weapon against it.

We are astonished at how clearly the fathers actually understood the physiological steps by which we become victims to these destructive viruses, these microbes of sin. How clearly the holy fathers understood that the soul and body are one unit and they operate together as a team; and how serious a Gnostic error it is to attempt to make a dichotomy between soul and body. Man does not *possess* a soul, but man *is* a living soul. Body and soul operate together and both are sanctified and both become deified and glorified together at one and the same time.

So, let us take a look at systematic prayer in relation to the physiological path by which sin enters into our mind and takes control, even becoming an addiction in us. We will see that, although the holy fathers did not know the physiological structure and pathways of the brain, they nevertheless understood very well how it operated, the steps by which temptation enters our mind and the stages by which it becomes manifested, develops and becomes habitual and then addictive. They told us that when sin first enters into our mind we have to be constantly on guard, guarding our mind like a watch-dog at the door. We have to always examine the things that enter into our mind so that the negative things not enter in and take root. We must even guard ourselves so that virtuous things not become sin in us. This is a part of a systematic prayer life, part of the healing process. "An ounce of prevention is worth a pound of cure" as the old English saying has it.

Here is the order by which, according to the holy fathers and mothers, sin enters into and takes possession of us.[5] When a **suggestion** enters into our mind, it is obviously not sin, because we have not acted upon it, we have not reacted in its favour. But, then, we begin to **contemplate** it. As we **contemplate** it, we find that we begin to **savour** and **take pleasure** in the suggestion. When we begin to take pleasure in the suggestion, even though we know just from our own human experience and reasoning — let alone the warnings of our conscience — that it can be destructive, we come to a point where we actually **accept** it in our mind. At what point does it become actual sin? At the point where we take pleasure in contemplating it or at the point where we accept it in our mind? At the point where we accept it, we come into a **conscious agreement**. At this point, we have decided not to struggle against it even though we know the consequences of not doing so. At this point, it becomes sin. Why does it become sin at that point? Because we have made a conscious decision to separate ourselves from God's will, we have rejected the rule and reign of God in our spiritual heart — our conscience — and this has separated us from God. This occurs not because it breaks a law, but because we have chosen to accept this over what we know to be God's will, and this separates us from God, causing us to "miss the mark" or "fall short of the goal" to which He has called us, for which He created us. Worse, we have rejected the terrible sacrifice which Christ made for us in order to liberate us from bondage to Satan, for we have made a conscious choice to enter back into that bondage. We have now set up a "golden calf" in our mind and returned again to the "hot pots of Egypt" (Ex.16:3). Still, even at this point our conscience calls out and rallies to our defence. We are faced with the choice of whether to reject the divine voice of our conscience or whether to heed it and struggle against our decision, our fall into sin. We are called upon at this point to *metanoia*, to repent — to rethink, to turn around and go in the opposite direction. The word repentance means to rethink, to have a different perspective on the matter. With regard to the guarding of our mind, when a suggestion enters our brain, we may not perceive it right away, but when it enters the part of our brain where we contemplate and think about it, then we are able to take action to drive it back out of our mind and to begin to resist it, or if it happens to be a virtuous thing then to accept it and try to set it into proper context, so that we are not led into sin through something that, on the surface, is virtuous. Ironically, we can lose our soul through our virtues also. So, we can think about it and we choose whether to accept or reject this thought or temptation. When we accept a negative impulse, it then becomes sin. That is why our Lord Jesus Christ said if one commits adultery in the mind, one is as guilty of it as if he committed it in the flesh. He did not mean that we are guilty for a passing thought, but you become guilty if you savour the thought of adultery, contemplating it in your mind and accept the idea. When you reconcile yourself to the idea, then you are guilty, because you have become reconciled to the act and accepted the desire and even carry out the deed in your imagination. You have resisted the voice of the conscience and failed to take steps to repulse the temptation. After that, as our mind takes this whole situation in, we act on it in one of two ways: either physically or mentally by contemplating and savouring it. Our conscience will still call us to turn back, to repent and will try to intervene in how we set the matter into context. When we set it in context, we adjust the context according to whether we heed our conscience or fight against it. If we have contextualized the matter contrary to our conscience, then it is on the way to becoming **habitual** and it is a small step from habitual to **addiction**. Our conscience continues to strive with us and at any stage we can turn back, but the further along the process we have gone, the more difficult the struggle becomes. When we set this whole matter into context, we either ignore our conscience or fall into a deep repentance about it and determine to purify our conscience through repentance and through prayer; seeking God's forgiveness — and actually we are seeking the forgiveness of our own conscience. The forgiveness of God is always there, if we just turn around and take hold of it. When we repent, we seek to reconcile our soul with our conscience. On the other hand, we might choose to push our conscience to the side. We think, "This is really very pleasurable. It does something for me; it might destroy somebody else and it might separate me from God, but it gives me pleasure, if only temporarily. I'm going to store it in this context in my memory so that I can draw it out again and savour it more."

Now we have contextualized it and stored it in our memory in a certain way so that, even without committing the deed physically, we can draw it from our memory and savour it and take pleasure in it, and so renew the sin. Instead of repenting and purifying our conscience and our mind, we corrupt both. Now we no longer need an external stimulus to lead us into the sin; we have a stored up internal stimulus and we lead ourselves into temptation. We do not need the devil to tempt us all the time. In fact, I think the devil sometimes stands in awe and envy at the effective way we can tempt ourselves. This is how we make the sin habitual, by drawing it out of our memory and not trying to cleanse our mind and our memory. The next stage is addiction and then hopeless bondage. And then we wonder what bondage it was that Jesus Christ wanted to redeem us from! Partly, the bondage of our own mind, as well as the bondage of Satan and the power of the fear of death. *"Inasmuch then as the children are partakers of flesh and blood, He also took part in the same; that through death He might destroy him that had the power of death, that is Satan, and deliver those who through fear of death were all their lives held in bondage"* (Hb. 2:14-15).

Man was all his lifetime held in bondage *by him, who had the power of death.* Not by God, but by the devil, and Satan has the power of death because we ourselves empower him. Satan has the power of spiritual death because we yield the power to him by accepting the delusions and deceit with which he entraps us. He has the power of physical death because physical death is the result of sin and we empower Satan by not struggling against sin. Mortality and death are not necessarily the same things. We have mortality and we do not necessarily have death. Man is not immortal by nature, but by the grace of God. Awareness of our mortality may help in the healing process of our nature so we can appreciate our mortality as something that reveals to us our need of God. Fear of death, however, bonds us to the spirit of this fallen world and the fallen nature. We die because we sin, we fall into sin because we fear death, and Satan is the great manipulator that makes us run on this treadmill to nowhere.

We have examined the concepts which the holy fathers used to describe the entry and progression of temptations into our mind. What is amazing is how closely this system equates the actual physiological process by which this takes place. I want to take a look at the brain and show you why, from a purely physiological point of view, systematized prayer is a part of the healing process, and why people who have a prejudice against systematized prayer, because they think it is dry formalism, are dead wrong.

When we talk in terms of human psychology and physiology, we discover the same process which the holy fathers described, only we use different terminology to describe it. Let us limit our discussion to negative impulses so that we will not become too technical. First of all, let us dispense with the idea that the physical heart is the seat, origin or generator of our emotions, temptations or emotional stimuli. All this takes place in the brain and the heart is only involved when increased bloodflow is mandated by the emotional reaction and called forth by the release of hormones.

Our reactions are the result of some impetus which, technically, is called a stimulus. We will speak about a visual stimulus — there could also be an auditory stimulus. Suppose we are walking along a path and suddenly we see that we are at the very edge of a cliff. We jump back suddenly and micro-seconds later we become aware of why we jumped back. This occurs so quickly that we are not conscious of the fact that fear preceded the awareness of fear and the reaction preceded the awareness of why we reacted. Here is what has happened, and this will be the circumstance in every case. It sounds very technical, but it all will make sense in a moment.

A stimulus enters the brain. What happens when a stimulus enters, through the eye in this case, is that, in our brain, the stimulus goes into a region called the "*thalamus*."

That is the little round thing sitting on top of the almond in the little drawing I have made here. Actually, it looks like a walnut, but it is called an "amygdala" which means "almond." The little golf ball sitting up there — like the sort of thing that keeps so many people out of church on Sunday morning — is the **thalamus**. The stimulus enters that part of the brain and then takes two directions: it goes up toward the top of the brain, toward the visual cortex and it also sends its signal down into the almond — the **amygdala**. It hits the almond first, and then we react automatically without thinking. We do not think about what it is we are doing, we just react, and that is very valuable, because if you are walking along a path and you start to teeter on the edge of a cliff, if you stop to think the whole thing out and reason what might happen if you fall over the cliff and hit the bottom, you will be down there before you react. Instead, you step back immediately, without thinking about it. Afterwards you go through the whole process of thinking it out, "Wow! That was a close call. I would have been smashed to bits if I fell over the cliff."

You start to reason about it instantly after the event, but you reacted emotionally before you thought out the matter. Then you go through the whole reasoning process, beginning from the visual cortex, and the whole picture forms. The reasoning or thinking process moves through the neo-cortex, and the signal, which began as an undefined stimulus, moves down to this lower part of the brain, down to the amygdala by a different route than the original signal from the thalamus. Now we are back down to the almond. Here, the two streams of the original stimulus meet in an area of the brain called the **hippocampus** — or hippocampi since there are two of them. Here, our brain sets the whole incident into context or **contextualizes** it, and prepares it to be sent into our memory. This is called **memory potentiation**, but we do not want to enter into a complex discussion of this. Since we have placed it in bold letters, however, you understand that it has a correlation in the system taught by the holy fathers, and we will place these two sets of vocabulary side by side in a moment so that you can see the true meaning and power of the patristic system of prayer defended by St Gregory Palamas. Forgetting about the cliff, let us look at a like sequence of events with a stimulus that might lead us into a sinful action. In that case, the conscience would have come into the action as soon as the stimulus moved from the thalamus to the cortex. As soon as we began to think about the meaning of the stimulus, our conscience would have entered into the deliberations in our brain.

Now, at the point where we contextualize the matter, the conscience enters into the process in a very powerful way. If we struggle to purify our relationship with our conscience,[6] to develop our conscience according to the faith and the principles of true morality, the conscience helps us to guard the mind from the very beginning of the appearance of this stimulus, which we might call a "temptation." It will help us to struggle against it at every stage, and now it helps us to set the whole thing into context. It brings us either to repentance or to going deeper into the abyss. Now the matter is set in context, we have two kinds of memory potentiation — long term and short term. If we have resisted our conscience and set this matter in the context of something that gives us plea-sure (even if we only accepted it in our minds and did not fulfil it physically), and we really want to hang on to and savour the contemplation of the deed, it is going to go into our long-term **memory** in much this set **context** and we can then draw it out of our own memory in order to savour it in future at the merest internal or external suggestion. So what happens now? We have a real potential for habitualization and addiction even if we do not fulfil the deed physically. We can become addicted to the contemplation of it. If you will compare this admittedly sketchy order of the steps by which a stimulus becomes action, context and

209

memory, with the stages of temptation given in the system of the holy fathers, you will see that they are the same. The holy fathers gave us something concrete and practical, not something merely theoretical or ethereal. They had an astonishing insight into the manner in which the mind works and the steps by which we fall into active sin. Having such under-standing, they also, with the grace of the Holy Spirit, provided us with systematic prayer to help prevent this fall or heal us after we had fallen. It is possible for humans to train themselves to take some control over the way they contextualize things for memory, and even to respond to many of their emotions in a reasoned way because human beings have a bi-directional neurosystem which allows the cortex to communicate with the limbic area of the brain. There are a number of approaches to psychotherapy in which this is demonstrated, and prayer is a part of our Orthodox Christian contribution to the psychotherapy process.[7]

Let us look at a more concrete example of the type of emotional response that might ultimately be contextualized and enter into active memory in a most destructive way. Our instant, emotional reaction to a stimulus can be useful, even life saving, as we have seen. The way we contextualize the matter can be quite destructive in some cases.

Anger arises from fear; there is no other source of anger except fear, even when anger is inculcated into us through propaganda. Fear is the mother of anger, and anger is the mother of hatred, and hatred is the mother of malice. Fear may be just an emotion that takes place without initial thought — as when we see a snake on the path just in front of us. Fear can elicit a fight or flight response from us and, in the case of a fight response, fear produces anger, which in turn helps us to fight more effectively. When we contextualize our fear, however, we can contextualize it as hate or submission or in a number of other ways. That is quite useful in case of a war. If you are afraid of the enemy and you have to fight against him it is much more effective if you hate him, because that way you can fight with more intensity and without reservations. That is why the propaganda machine of any nation in the war tries to build up a fear of the enemy and then turn that fear into hatred. That is why they demonize the enemy, so that we will hate him and have less qualms about shooting him. It is also useful if the head of the government or the head of state wants to control you, because they can manipulate you far easier through fear than through any other emotion. Hitler spent a long time building up fear of the Jews so he could turn it into a hatred so that the nation would support him, no matter what he did. Hitler became the one who was going to "save us from this great enemy who was destroying our society and our culture," namely the Jews. Any time a demagogue wants to manipulate us or control us, he first has to make us afraid of someone in society, some group. It does not matter which group, but anybody who is a scapegoat.

And then you change that fear into a hatred. The demagogue then presents himself as the one who has the solution, who can lead us against this enemy who might otherwise destroy our society and our culture and all that we hold dear. History has shown us how such a demagogue can take control of people and lead them into hatred and terrible deeds. It does not matter whether it is Hitler or a televangelist; the method and the end result might be the same.

Satan is the master demagogue. He can lead us to fear someone, and then to hate them, and then into the bondage of malice. In such a state, we can become most destructive. Our conscience will try to intervene in this process at many stages and turn it back, even after it has entered into our memory to hate such and such a person or group of people. Our conscience will call upon us to repent of our hatred or malice and be healed of it. Alas, we can be a demagogue to ourselves, and in such a case, healing is even more difficult because we have to pray for help in overcoming ourselves. Our systematized prayer, the patristic hesychastic prayer defended by Saint Gregory Palamas in particular, serves to deliver and heal us at every stage of the process. Why is this prayer so potent in this healing process? Because it is focused,[8] it has a known "destination," and it is aimed at a specific, practical purpose. We know the process and the steps by which temptation and sin enter and are manifested in our minds, and Orthodox Christian prayer is designed by experience and grace to precisely respond to this process.

Orthodox Christian prayer is a "prescription" given by the Holy Spirit, designed to help in healing us of the spiritual viruses and microbes that want to parasitically inhabit our flesh and bring it into bondage and cause that spiritual illness which leads to spiritual death.

Our brain, created by God to house our mind, is an integral part of our being, the seat of our reasoning faculties, the locus of our emotions and the dwelling place of our conscience, our spiritual heart. It is the place where we must begin the healing process. Hesychastic prayer is a spiritual medication. It is a process by which we gain control of the stimuli that enter our mind; it helps us to assess them and limit them and ultimately, such prayer helps greatly in the healing of our mind, the purification of the conscience and the strengthening of the will. It involves both the body and the mind, and so helps to collect us and unify our spirit. Prayer is psychotherapy — the treatment of the soul. Such systematized prayer is an extremely important part of Christian life, because Christian life is a struggle to find healing for the whole being, the whole person.

7
SYSTEMATIC PRAYER
AND THEOSIS
The Existential Goal of the
Orthodox Christian Prayer Life

Prayer also helps to bring us into accord with the will of God so that we no longer fall short of the "mark" or "goal," which is to be united with God and share in His immortality, in everlasting life and eternal joy. Everyone who has sinned has fallen short of the glory of God. We fall short of that glory of God which He desires that we participate in through *theosis* — the glory of God, not the "glorious ideal that God has for us," as some sectarian versions of the Bible say, but literally the glory of God (2Pet.1:4;[9] 2Cor.3:18). We attain this state of participation in the glory of God by ascending through purification to illumination and then to glorification. Prayer is the primary instrument for this ascent because prayer is an act of seeking to draw near to God just as it is a tool for overcoming our sinful separation from God.

Everybody in the Church is called "saint" by Apostle Paul because the Hebrew and Greek equivalents of the word indicate "dedicated to," "set apart," "sanctified to the use of." Yet we have those people whom we uniquely call "saints" and place on icons in a transfigured form.

To understand this, and to understand the essence of Christian struggle, let us first set aside the un-Orthodox idea of "canonizing" saints. We do not canonize saints in the Orthodox Church. This idea of "canonization" is not an Orthodox Christian concept, but a term borrowed from the Latins. The expression in the Orthodox Church is *glorification*.

The goal and destination of our prayer life and

struggle is this ascent through purification of the conscience to illumination in the grace of the Holy Spirit, to glorification so that we no longer "fall short of the glory of God." How do we know that a person has attained to glorification, except that it be revealed to us by the Holy Spirit? And why is that revealed to us by the Holy Spirit, except that it shows that it is possible for man to attain? Why do we venerate those glorified saints in the Church, except that they have proved to us that though we have fallen short or missed the mark of the glory of God, we can return to that glory and ascend to that *"prize of the high calling of God in Christ Jesus"* being *"changed into the same image from glory to glory by the Spirit of the Lord" (Phil.3:14; 2 Cor.3:18)*, and can participate in the glory of God; that we can become truly dwelling places and temples of the Holy Spirit; and that the Holy Spirit can abide in us and work though us, as He does in the saints. In such a way, people can see the glory of God and desire it. Only by this witness can mankind comprehend that our Lord Jesus Christ became man in order to unify man with God in Himself, and understand that our redemption consists in making it possible for us to truly participate in, and attain to, the glory of God once more — through the process of *theosis*.

8
PRAYER AND THE
HEALING OF OUR NATURE;
The Wholeness of Man;
Order in Place of Chaos

The most concrete life of prayer, and systematic prayer in particular, is hesychastic prayer — the prayer defended by Saint Gregory Palamas and the prophetic ministry. It is a healing process by which our fallen human nature can become collected and focused, delivered from chaos and redirected toward the goal for which God created us. By means of such focused prayer, we can once more assimilate to our hearts the principles of life revealed to us by our Creator and Redeemer. With the help of divine grace, such prayer can help us conquer those things that separate us from God and from one another. By means of such an active and focused prayer life we can, with the grace of the Holy Spirit, become healed of those spiritual microbes, viruses and build-ups of spiritual cholesterol in our system. Consequently, when one denigrates or denies that systematic or hesychastic prayer which is fundamental to Orthodoxy, one denigrates the Gospel itself. Only the spiritually blind or ignorant could consider as formalistic ritualism that system of prayer which leads us toward such a definite goal, a definite destination, toward our high calling in Jesus Christ, toward restoration to participation in the glory of God. This is precisely what systematic prayer is doing for us. It is not a magical process; it is a free will act of setting our desire toward purity, true morality and unity with God. The action of such a free struggle in man, and the process of such ordered prayer, helps to collect and bring the whole person together, dispelling the chaos and confusion from our lives. It solidifies our "person" and draws it into true communion with Christ. God is not a demagogue or a dictator; He does not force us into anything. The idea of predestination is a Gnostic heresy. There is no predestination for man just as there is no determinism in the created universe. We are free moral beings and, as such, obliged to make our own free will decisions concerning our relationship with God and our expectations for everlasting life. Nowhere in creation do we find predestination or determinism. The Heisenberg Principle of Uncertainty and the Hamiltonian Principle, which is the vector operator of the universe itself, testify to this. God created the universe as well as us. The universe is not something that came to be accidentally, and the structure of the universe is not accidental and we, as part of that created universe, are intimately connected to it. Thus, there is no predestination or determinism anywhere in the universe and least of all in the matter of mankind's salvation. So, we have to make free choices. God does not hold us like puppets on a string. We have the capacity to love and to reject love, so we can have a spousal relationship or opt for sheer ego. In this, we can understand the relationship between humanity and

God. Both the Old and the New Testament covenants between God and man are spousal relationships, not legal agreements. That is why the Church is called the Bride of Christ. That is why God would refer to the old Israel, when it fell away into idolatry and Ecumenism with other nations as an adulteress or a harlot, because it was a violation of a spousal relationship — of the sacred covenant.

9
THE POWER OF COMMON OR UNIFIED SYSTEMATIC PRAYER

The life of prayer, hesychastic prayer in particular, is the healing process which the Holy Spirit has revealed to man. By means of it, we cooperate with God's grace and gradually attain the healing of our fallen nature. We begin the process first by guarding the mind with prayer and vigilance, and then by entering into ourselves and looking after the soul itself as a garden, something like the garden of Eden. We enter into the garden of our soul to tend it, to pull out the weeds and tares which pollute it and choke off the fruitful crops of love and virtue. By means of this loving and prayerful cultivation, we make the soul a fit dwelling place for the Holy Spirit. When we seek to acquire the indwelling of the Holy Spirit, we seek the help of that same Spirit to prepare ourselves for its indwelling. By continually tending the temple of our bodies and the garden of our souls, we attain purity of conscience so that we are able to bear the illumination of the Holy Spirit. We have to remember the promise, "blessed are those who love the beauty of God's house," and consider our soul and body together to be, as the Apostle says, His temple. If God's house is going to be our heart, our soul, our person, we have to constantly be tending that temple, and our life of prayer is precisely about such a cleansing and beautifying of this "temple" of God.

Systematic prayer is dealing with this whole aspect of our life. We can pour out our prayers in moments of grief and lamentation, like the prophet Jeremiah, or in times of personal joy from the depths of own hearts. Systematic prayer is not only a personal, hesychastic experience, however. More powerful still is that unified prayer of the worshipping community when we all come together in the Divine Liturgy to pour out our common prayer. Such common prayer is like an army marching in unison. When soldiers are marching together, in step, such unified marching has great force. If the soldiers come to a bridge, they have to break step so that they are no longer marching in unison and rhythm, otherwise the strength of the unified step will cause the bridge to collapse. Our common, unified, systematic prayer has such power because it unites our hearts, draws us into a love and oneness with our neighbours and focuses us as a family, a worshipping community, on our ultimate destination, our common hope. It is true that God knows what we need before we ask and that God is always present to us. Our struggle is to become present to God. The Apostle never said, "Find some way to make God become reconciled to you," but, "Be ye reconciled to God."[10] God is always reconciled to us, He does not change His attitude toward us, but we need to be reconciled to Him. Our common prayer, which brings us together in a common act of love and worship, opens to us the experience of love of neighbour and unity with them in the grace of the Holy Spirit. You cannot obey the word of Scripture to *have love among yourselves* if you are alone. If it is only you alone, there is no one to have love among. You can only have such love in a community, and never more than when we worship as a community. God calls us together as family, as community. The whole structure of the universe is based on the principle of a hierarchical family and community. Even galaxies do not exist in isolation, but they exist in clusters of galaxies. So, everything in the universe is set to rhythms and harmonies and structures that indicate community, that indicate family. Consequently, we pray together in the Divine Liturgy in a way that informs and illumines the heart as part of a worshipping community, and a family of believers.

The Divine Liturgy is revelation and prophecy given to us in the context of community. Just as in the Old Testament, the structure of the Temple was a revelation and prophecy, so every aspect of our common, systematic, communal prayer is a revelation to us. After all, the Holy of Holies was a type of

Paradise. And it was in both Paradise and in the Holy of Holies that God the Word came personally to be present with man. It is the New Testament temple, where the altar is equally a type of Paradise, that God constantly calls us back to Paradise.

The curtain of the Temple was torn in two at the crucifixion of Christ, because the Cross was the key that unlocked the gates of Paradise. The curtain was a type of that gate of Paradise which was no longer closed against us, but was reopened now, through Christ. That is why, when we begin the Divine Liturgy, we open the royal gates, because the gates of Paradise are opened to us. How are they opened and by what means are we called to enter in? As soon as the royal gates are opened, the priest elevates the Gospel and makes the sign of the Cross with it saying, "Blessed is the Kingdom of Father, Son, and Holy Spirit." The Cross is the key that unlocked the gates of Paradise and the Gospel is the voice that calls us to enter into that kingdom that is now revealed before us.

The Gospel is only useful, however, if people understand it, and decide to actually live it and not just pay lip service to it. It enters into our hearts and transforms us, but it actually changes us only when we make a conscious effort to assimilate it and be changed by it. The way we bring the Gospel into our hearts to transform us and to change us is *through prayer*. However, it must be prayer that is informed by the Gospel, prayer that is filled with the living *spirit* of the Gospel and not the letter only. This is a systematic

221

prayer, not just the emotional prayer that we sometimes pour out in times of need, though these do indeed, bring us into a relationship with God.

The systematic prayer which the Holy Spirit has revealed to us in the Church, and which was so diligently defended by Saint Gregory Palamas, makes the Gospel deeply alive within us. This is so because we do it intentionally, we do it consciously, we do it knowing why we are doing it; we do it knowing what destination we are aiming for, what goal we are aspiring to, what healing and restoration we are seeking. It is a prayer planned, planted, and tended, because we know where we want to go and we lay down the road map before us. Sin enters into us and develops in us systematically, as we have seen, and so we turn it back and drive it out systematically. And that is how we actually get to our destination. Even when we practise the systematic prayer of the Church alone, we are still practising the common prayer of the community, though there is no substitute for the Liturgical prayer of the "synaxis" — the coming together of the community. "One Christian is no Christian," the desert fathers often said. You cannot have love for one another if you are egoistic and alone. You can only have love for one another in community. It is because of both this profound sense of community and this awareness of a personal place in the community that we give a child of forty days Holy Communion *by name* immediately after baptism. They receive Communion by name as do all members of the community because, having entered into a spousal relationship with God in the Church, they have a name in the community, a name before God. When children receive Communion by name, they learn from their youngest infancy and begin to understand that they have a name before God, and therefore a personal relationship with Him, and a value in the community. They grow up realizing that they are a living, vital part of the worshipping community, they are a royal priesthood. They participate in the system of communal worship and prayer even when they are crying or appear inattentive in Church. They receive Communion by name, because they have a name before the throne of God, a name that is written in the Lamb's Book of Life. They are able to understand the connection with the community and with God through the community. Our life of prayer, our life of systematic prayer establishes that community of believers and brings us together as one through Liturgy and gives us a common face before God, and a real sense that God is our common Father.

This brings us back full circle to the Lord's prayer, and we understand why God is our Father. Because we are a community, a family, God reveals Himself as our Father, so that we can understand ourselves as family. "Our Father Who art in the Heavens;" our Father, because we are a community, a family, brought together by the power and grace of the Holy Spirit. Our Lord Jesus Christ established us as a family by accepting us as His brethren.[11] Jesus Christ is not ashamed to call us His brothers and sisters and, therefore, we are not afraid to call God our Father. We are a community and a family, otherwise God is not our Father. A family is not made up of isolated individuals. If we are isolated individuals we have no common mother and no common father. God will not be our Father by different spouses, for we are not stepchildren, stepbrothers, stepsisters. We have a common mother, even the Church, and the spouse of the Church is our common Father. God has revealed Himself to us through that family and community, and His covenant through the mystery of marriage. The mystery of redemption is revealed through the mystery of marriage. The covenant with God is a spousal relationship, not a legal agreement, and the mystery of redemption is the mystery of co-suffering love, the co-suffering of the Father with His children. The co-suffering love of God with His creation is what makes our restoration and redemption possible. It offers a bond of the most perfect and powerful love, a love that is willing to lay down its life even for those who despise it. The systematic prayer of Orthodox Christianity is a prayer life that is meaningful and understood, prayer that has a reason, prayer that has a destination, prayer that has a purpose; this is a healing process that has been given to us by God so that we might come into accord with His love and assimilate it to ourselves by defeating those sinful barriers to it which develop within us. This is the very meaning of systematic prayer, and of hesychastic prayer in particular.

This is the whole root of the "hesychastic controversy." The whole controversy between Orthodox Christianity and Western Augustinianism concerned our relationship with God, our ability to know God through His uncreated *Energy*, our ability to have a personal relationship with God, not through types and symbols, but directly through Jesus Christ. It was about our ability to be restored to the glory of God, our ability through prayer, through systematic prayer, to find that healing and restoration which Jesus Christ has made possible for us — the healing of the fallen human nature. That is why we know that the monks and nuns who went away into the desert were not simply seeking isolation away from the rest of humanity, forgetting about the plight of the world and mankind. We all have a common human nature. When one person, through prayer, struggles to purify their human nature and bring it into accord with the life of Jesus Christ, they become filled with light. When they become more light and less darkness in themselves, they drive the darkness out of their own life, they invite the light into their own life. When they accomplish this, then because there is less darkness in them, there is less darkness in the whole human nature and there is more light in the human nature. Their victory is a victory for all of humanity — especially those who believe. So, the monastics in the farthest part of the desert, Saint Sarah sitting on top of her house, Saint Pelagia in her little kellia, Saint Anthony the Great, Abba Sisoes or Abba Justin Popovich at Chelia, all these holy fathers and mothers were struggling for the healing and redemption of the whole human nature. In physics this is called the principle of non-locality. Everything that occurs in one field of the universe effects all the universe, every other field of the universe. Just so, every saint who has achieved glorification has an impact on all the rest of the fallen human nature. All the rest of the fallen human nature is more filled with light, and less filled with darkness, because one person has attained glorification. This is why we venerate the saints and this is why it is such a catastrophe that some people thought that there was something wrong with venerating them. They never understood the principles at work and they never understood the true meaning of redemption.

I want to close by going back to this first statement which is written on the board. Is morality a heresy? Morality is a heresy when it becomes a substitute for our life in Christ. Morality becomes a substitute for our life in Christ when we reduce religion to a moral code, when we reduce the faith to a system of correct behaviour instead of an existential struggle to purify the conscience and acquire the indwelling of the Holy Spirit. We cannot acquire the Holy Spirit by means of correct behaviour, which is just a matter of human works and legalistic works at that. Such an approach fills us with so much judgment and condemnation and arrogance and self-righteousness that the Holy Spirit remains alien to us. We begin to think ourselves to be moral and everyone who is not like us somehow immoral. We set ourselves as the criterion of morality, but there can be no true morality without the inner transformation of our person. Perfect holiness consists only in perfect love, not in correct behaviour. Righteousness does not consist in correct behaviour, but in genuine co-suffering love and pure faith. No deed has any moral value unless it proceeds from the heart motivated by love. Otherwise it is simply ethical or correct behaviour according to one or another system of law — a human work which anyone in any culture, with or without faith in God can attain to. The Old Testament law could help to preserve society but it could not save anyone, no matter how diligently they fulfilled it to the letter. Moreover, since it could not transform the heart, it could not even preserve the nation from falling constantly away from God. Our Lord Jesus Christ, the only One who fulfilled perfect righteousness was motivated solely by love, co-suffering love. And that is why our Lord Jesus Christ became our righteousness on the Cross, and imputed that righteousness to us through faith. Only righteousness is the fulfilment of the law and righteousness consists only in perfect love. The self-righteousness, the arrogance that we have which makes us judge and condemn others, by which we put our foot on the heads of the weak and push them deeper into darkness by our arrogance — this is the apex of unrighteousness and it is a great sin. That is ultimately what our struggle of prayer is all about, trying to acquire perfect, co-suffering love in ourselves, becoming truly conformed to the image of Christ, so that we may actually share in His glory, the glory of the Living God, receiving by grace through faith, *"the prize of the high calling of God in Christ Jesus." being "changed into the same image from glory to glory by the Spirit of the Lord" (Phil .3:14; 2 Cor.3:18).*

ENDNOTES:

[1]. Paper presented at the St Gregory Palamas Conference by Dr. Anastasios Papademetriou.

[2]. Moralism and morality are not synonyms. Moralism is a form of external conformity, used as an excuse to persecute or degrade people whom the moralist feels are not living up to his or her standards of external proper behaviour. Morality is an inner struggle to purify the heart so that our external behaviour is motivated by a sincere inner love, with no external show, boasting or berating of others.

[3]. The New Age Movement trivializes this by turning it into a pantheistic concept.

[4]. Ecumenism is a form of reductionism and minimalism. Many Orthodox leaders have been more than willing to compromise the faith for it and to trivialize even the concept of "truth," not to mention the sufferings of the holy martyrs.

[5]. [Editor's Note]: Vladika Lazar gave this talk extemporaneously, without prepared notes. I have added emphases to the steps he describes from the system of the holy fathers in describing the steps by which sin develops in us, and also to the steps by which a stimulus enters the mind and develops, from the clinical description Vladika gives for comparison. The

emphases make the comparison clearer. I have also added Scripture verse locations to most of his quotations from the Bible.

[6]. See *The Purification of the Conscience*, by Archbishop Lazar Puhalo in the Synaxis Press Point of Faith series.

[7]. I hasten to add that it is not a replacement for treatment by a competent psychiatrist. Priests should never delude themselves that they can guide a person's psychotherapy by themselves, without the primary treatment by a psychiatrist.

[8]. Focus is so critical for our spiritual life. Orthodox Christian systematic prayer, both hesychastic (the "Jesus Prayer") and the prayers of the Liturgical cycle and the Prayer Book, serve to focus our lives and our spiritual struggle. When our Lord Jesus Christ said *"strait is the gate, and narrow is the way, which leadeth unto life, and few there be that find it. (Mt.7:14)*, He was speaking about focus. The narrow gate and path are visible to those who have focus in their spiritual lives, who have set a clear destination for themselves and focused their lives on it.

[9]. *Whereby are given unto us exceeding great and precious promises: that by these ye might be partakers of the divine nature.*

[10]. 2Cor.5:18-20.

[11]. Hb.2:11.

APPENDIX
PLATONISTIC ESSENTIAL-
ISM

We should say something more about why Platonistic essentialism is not acceptable to us. Let me begin with Aquinas, however (Aristotelian though he was). For Aquinas, essentialism is the coming into being or manifestation in substance of a potentiality. A substance is an essence which has been given existence. In a way, this Aristotelianism was an improvement over Plato's *kosmos noetos* — the transcendent realm of Forms or Ideals which are archetypes of everything in time. Aristotle's improvement lies in the fact that he recognises the Forms naturally in *this* world. For example, he considers the acorn to be the Form of the oak tree rather than placing an abstract ideal Form in a transcendent cosmos. For Plato, anything that has physical existence is a "Form" (or "Idea") which has received matter. Essence is seen as a preexisting "Form" or, perhaps more correctly, an Ideal Form with the potential of physical manifestation. Some existentialist (such as Husserl,[1] who also had strong Rationalist tendencies), extend this so that essence is the potentiality for the manifestation of any act, deed or act of will, void of the context of the act.

Socrates (who was Plato's teacher) expressed the

concept of essence as an "idea," or a "criterion." Plato, particularly in *The Republic*, extends or explains essentialism with his idea of archetypal, ideal Forms preexisting in a transcendent realm. At this point, we have to consider the term "*universals*," which would occupy so much energy of debate in the Middle Ages. "*Universals*" were only names or the nomenclature of ideas, but because of "essentialism," the concept formed the basis of debate between Aristotelians and Platonists, Nominalists and Realists. We do not want to discuss these debates here, but they do reflect on why we assert the weakness of "essentialism." A quill pen is such because it is a copy of the Form or has the "universal" expression of "quillness." Forms which have been defined are prototypes or archetypes of things which are seen, which bear the same name. Things which are seen or experienced in the realm of sense perception are copies of Forms which have been named. To know the essence of something is to know the defined archetype of it. This is reminiscent of the principle of First Cause in which some real aspect of efficient cause (*causa efficiens*) passes into the entity of the effect. Indeed, the Realists believed that *universals* are ontologically real while, in fact, they are only a semantic convention, a way of classifying things. But now I have mixed Plato and Aristotle together and I am not completely certain where the boundary actually begins and ends, so we will leave it as a general critique of "essentialism". We might say that we do not accept Plato's essentialism because we do not accept

231

his concept of the ideal Forms in the *kosmos noetos.*

ENDNOTES:

[1]. Edmund Husserl (1859-1938). Founder of the Phenomenology concept. He was a Rationalist and used some of the same approaches as Kant, nevertheless, his thought was also Existentialist.

INDEX

234

Goa, David J. 41,
Gospel rock 46,
Grace 8-12, 14-16, 18, 22, 26, 28, 29, 41, 42, 58, 65, 68, 69, 71, 73, 75, 80-82, 86, 89-92, 102, 109, 113, 116, 118, 119, 121, 122, 125, 128
Grant, George 145,
Greek Orthodox Theological Review 61, 62
Gregory of Nyssa 78,
Gregory Palamas 62, 63, 87, 88, 90, 92, 103, 112, 115, 119, 124, ,
Hadas, Dr. Moses 6
Hammurabi 130,
Hari Krishna 53,
Health care 27
Heaven 16, 17, 30, 31, 76, 95 -100, 136
Heaven and Hell 30
Heavenly Kingdom 43, 45, 76, 77, 83,
Hegel, Georg W.F. 40
Heidegger, Martin 2
Hell 16, 31
Hellenism 30
Herd behaviour 22
Heredity 13
Hesychastic 90, 91, 93, 103, 115, 116, 119-121, 126,
Hesychastic prayer 90, 91, 93, 103, 115, 116, 119, 120, 126,
Hesychastic renewal 90,
Hilary of Arles 62,
Hilary of Poitiers 62,
Hippocampus 112,
Hitler, Adolf 91, 115,
Holiness 14, 17, 21, 56, 128, 146
Holy fathers 17, 50, 67, 94, 103-106, 109, 110, 112, 113, 127
Holy nation 17, 19
Holy One 17
Holy Spirit 3, 9, 11, 14, 15, 22, 29, 42, 51, 58, 59, 63, 67, 69, 70, 72, 77, 81, 82, 85, 89-92, 100, 102, 113, 116,

118-123, 125, 127, 144, 146,
Holy Trinity 39, 41, 67, 80, 81
Hormones 99, 110,
Human nature 3, 7, 8, 10-12, 74, 75, 85, 91, 102, 103, 119, 126, 127, 130, 141
sanctified 10
Humanism 62,
Humanity 25
Hume, David 139, 141, 143
Husserl, Edmund 147
Hydrogen atom 43
Hypermoralism 13, 91
hypostasis 5-12, 40, 51, 58, 140
Hypostatically 12
Hypothalamus 18, 29
Iconography 46, 53
Ideal forms 24
Idolatrous 40
Ignatios the Godbearer 62
Illumination 14, 39
Image 13
Immortal 11, 111
Immortality 11, 119
industrial revolution 62
Introduction to Saint Gregory Palamas 62
Irenae of Lyons 62
Isaak of Nineveh 31
Israel 17
James 56, 64, 65, 69, 81
Jeremiah 121
Jesus Christ 19
John Cassian 62
John Chrysostom 33, 62, 65, 83
John Damascene 63, 142
Judaeo-Christian tradition 60, 61
Juridicalism 30
Justin Popovich at Chelia 127
Justin the New of Serbia 63
Kalomiros, Dr. Alexandre 32
kamikaze 136
Kane, Dr. Robert Hilary 132, 133, 137, 139, 143

237

238

Made in the USA
Coppell, TX
16 July 2021